Classic Diners of
MASSACHUSETTS

Classic Diners of MASSACHUSETTS

LARRY CULTRERA

Charleston | London

THE
History
PRESS

Published by The History Press
Charleston, SC 29403
www.historypress.net

917.44 CUL

Front cover: *top left*: Al Mac's Diner interior; *top right*: Capitol Diner; *center left*: Miss Mendon
Diner; *center right*: Salem Diner; *bottom left*: Miss Florence Diner; *bottom right*: Miss Florence
Diner interior.
Back cover: *top left*: Wheelhouse Diner sign; *top center*: Route 9 Diner; *top right*: Rosebud Diner
interior; *bottom*: Rosebud Diner.
All images are by the author unless otherwise noted.

First published 2011

Manufactured in the United States

ISBN 978.1.60949.323.3

Library of Congress CIP data applied for.

Notice: The information in this book is true and complete to the best of our knowledge. It is
offered without guarantee on the part of the author or The History Press. The author and
The History Press disclaim all liability in connection with the use of this book.

Contents

Foreword

For more than thirty years, Larry Cultrera has been in the front line of the trenches—the diner trenches—observing, photographing, sharing and writing about the comings and goings in the world of diners.

Before the Internet, even looking for diners was a long and laborious process. There were the Yellow Pages; there was word of mouth from diner owners and patrons, who always had a recommendation for the next place down the road. A network was slowly built of East Coast enthusiasts who were fascinated with all things diner. Lists were assembled: Larry had his logbooks and his photographs; I had my card catalogue and my slides. We noted the basics: address, manufacturer, year of construction, serial number, details of former names or locations and maybe some information on the owner.

Diners are in Larry's blood. He is a major contributor to the overall mission of all diner enthusiasts: to keep the institution thriving while maintaining an ever-growing record of what has been lost.

Larry delights in telling of his recent finds: his meeting with the granddaughter of Peter Calimaris, longtime owner of three diners in Quincy, and a previously unknown image of a Valentine Diner, Howard Rust's Radamat, that was built in Kansas and was once located in Larry's hometown of Medford. He is often the first to know of diners on the move. When the Bel-Aire Diner was jacked off its foundation on Route 1, the Newburyport Turnpike, in Peabody and shifted to the back of the lot to make way for a new development, Larry was the first to spot it. On August 19, 1993, he reported that the Boulevard Diner, stored for two years at O.B. Hill's Natick trucking facility, was moving to Carteret, New Jersey, to be refurbished by the Musi Dining Car Company before heading off to London.

For many years, I was a privileged recipient of this information. I got to hear it first. And even now, with his blog, he often lets me know news firsthand before it is posted.

In June 1993, when the Society for Commercial Archeology (SCA) held its "Diner Experience," a weekend conference in Philadelphia, Larry was the first speaker on the program. In fact, he has been giving talks on diners for decades to groups large and small at historical societies and libraries throughout New England. It is a way of connecting with the locals who come to reminisce about what has disappeared from the landscape or to find out what happened to an old favorite spot.

Long before the advent of blogs, Larry disseminated his knowledge through a regular feature, "Diner Hotline," in the publications of the SCA. Through these efforts, he became the clearinghouse for facts and rumors concerning the world of diners: what's open, what's closed, what's threatened, what's changed hands, what's been bricked over, what's newly discovered. "Diner Hotline" was fantastic, but his devoted readers had to wait months for the subsequent edition, and he was limited by space in a print magazine. So "Diner Hotline" went digital, and Larry truly came into his own. Using his reporting skills, his large library of photos, his expertise at scanning and Photoshop and his anecdotal style, he brings his blog (dinerhotline. wordpress.com) to life.

Larry also uses his design talents to build life-like scale models of some of his favorite diners and to design graphics for diner clients. He was also instrumental in preparing the shop drawings for the rehabilitation of the Four Sisters Owl Diner in Lowell.

Since we first met, over a cup of coffee at the counter of the Apple Tree Diner in Dedham in the early 1980s, Larry has been an unflagging supporter of the institution of diners. Now, in this book, he has brought his expertise to bear upon the diners of the Commonwealth of Massachusetts. We are all richer through his knowledge.

Richard J.S. Gutman
West Roxbury, Massachusetts

Acknowledgements

T hanks to my friend Steven T. Repucci, the guy who started going on short Sunday morning road trips with me back in 1979. I recall at the start of that first excursion how we decided to have breakfast at Genia's Diner in North Woburn, right around the corner from where Steve was residing at the time. In fact, we did that for two or three weeks in a row until we got the bright idea to start going to different diners, which would then determine the direction of the ride each week thereafter.

I also want to thank the pioneers in the field of diner research whom I consider the "first wave," the people who led the way for the rest of us diner freaks to follow. First and foremost, Richard J.S. Gutman, whose college thesis ultimately evolved into the 1979 book *American Diner*. This book was later updated and expanded into the Bible of diner history published in 1993 entitled *American Diner Then & Now*. Dick more recently authored an Images of America book called *The Worcester Lunch Car Company* and, along with his wife, Kellie O. Gutman, has been putting together multimedia presentations and curated museum exhibits on the subject of diners for close to forty years. Also a huge part of the first wave is John Baeder, whose seminal 1978 book *Diners*, filled with his wonderful stories, sketches and paintings, was a total inspiration. I cherish both Dick and John's continued friendship for the last thirty years. I cannot forget Donald Kaplan and Allyson Bellink, coauthors of the first book I purchased in 1980, *Diners of the Northeast*. This book fueled the nascent feelings to fever pitch that snowballed and continues to this day.

Thanks also to David Hebb, with whom I crossed paths two or three times in the early days on the diner trail. Dave was out there at least two years prior to me, documenting diners with his photographs. He soon became another travel companion sharing numerous miles and experiences, as well as information, over the years. Many other diner enthusiasts have come along since I started this journey, and quite a few have made my life richer for knowing them. At the top of that list would be Brian Butko, who for years helped make my "Diner Hotline" column in the Society for Commercial Archeology's (SCA) *Journal* magazine what it was.

Others who have shared the journey include Randy Garbin, whose *Roadside Magazine* and later website (Roadside Online) helped to further the cause and rally many a kindred spirit to document their own travels along the highways and byways. I also want to thank Rich Beaubien, Becky Haletky, Stephen Lintner, Christine Guedon-DeConcini, Glenn Wells, Mike Engle, Gary Thomas, Denise J.R. Bass, Paula Walsh, Gordon Tindall, Michael Stewart, Spencer Stewart, Colin Strayer and Beth Lennon, who have all been out in the trenches documenting diners and other roadside-related places, as well as being sounding boards or travel companions. I cannot forget all the regular readers of my Diner Hotline Weblog, some of whom go all the way back to the hard copy version in the *SCA Journal*, and Michael Karl Witzel, who asked me to write the foreword for his book, *The American Diner*, back in 1999.

Special thanks to my cousin John Gonnella and his wife, Evelyn, for their help with providing the interior shots of Tony's Café, as well as all the background info. Thanks also to Kathleen Kelly Broomer for her input on the National Register information. I'd like to extend my gratitude to all the diner owners past and present who have helped me with some of the personal history and information for this book. Among those owners there have been many over the years whom I feel honored to call my friends. The top of this list includes Bob Fennell of the Capitol Diner, Bill Nichols and Helen DeFransisco of the Rosebud Diner, Phil and Celeste Paleologos of the Shawmut Diner, Tim Kamataris of Tim's Diner and Arthur Bombadier of Tex Barry's Coney Island Diner, as well as Chris and Matt Blanchard of Blanchard's 101 Diner. Former owners who have helped are Charles and Nicholas Georgenes of Victoria's Diner, John Kallas of Salem Diner and John and Sue Barrett of Buddy's Diner. There were two other former diner owners who I was very close to early on and for many years: Warren Jones of the Apple Tree Diner and Owen Abdalian of the Main Street Diner. Both Warren and Owen passed away in the last ten years, and I truly miss them and their presence in my life.

ACKNOWLEDGEMENTS

I would also like to acknowledge Jeff Saraceno and the crew at The History Press. Jeff found my blog on the Internet and contacted me to inquire if I might be interested in writing a book on diners.

Finally, thanks to all my family and friends who have encouraged me but most of all to my wife, Denise, who has gone above and beyond the call of duty, putting up with this obsession for the last twenty years.

Introduction

My interest in diners goes back to when I was five or six years old. I loved to go on car rides with my family and was very observant, looking at every roadside building that we passed along the way. My dad, Sebastian R. "Sam" Cultrera, loved driving, and I remember one day when he said we were going on a short ride, we actually ended up at the other end of the state in the Berkshire Hills along the Mohawk Trail. Now that was my kind of ride! I have a distinct memory of asking my dad about a particular building we used to pass by in my hometown of Medford, Massachusetts, the Star Lite Diner on Mystic Avenue. I recall inquiring if it was a railroad car, and my dad told me no, not quite, that it was a type of restaurant called a diner that was built in a factory and that the factories did in fact design them to resemble railroad cars. By the summer of 1965, when I was twelve years old, I was helping out at the family business, a store that sold meats and a small amount of groceries called the Blue Eagle Market. Dad's usual routine was to head into the wholesale meat markets in Boston to get supplies, and on the way we would stop for breakfast at places like the Star Lite Diner and Bobbie's Diner, both in Medford. Other places we stopped at were the White Tower in Somerville and Victoria's Diner in Boston. These breakfast stops gave me a great appreciation for diners that carried over to my adulthood. Dad was still around when I began to photograph diners and collect memorabilia in 1980. He always enjoyed looking at my photos or a new addition to my diner postcard collection and never asked me why I was doing this—he instinctively knew.

INTRODUCTION

After graduating from high school, I had some great times hanging out at Carroll's Colonial Dining Car (also in Medford) with my friends in the early to late 1970s. Carroll's was centrally located and was a fantastic meeting spot that operated twenty-four hours a day and was always busy, especially after all the bars and nightclubs were closed. There was usually a line out the door waiting to get in at 2:30 or 3:00 a.m. By 1979, when Steve Repucci and I started our Sunday morning road trips, I was aware that Steve, like me, enjoyed stopping at diners for breakfast, and a new weekly tradition was born. I was also influenced by Steve to get into 35mm photography and got the bright idea to start documenting the diners we saw in our travels. Thus, on November 29, 1980, I took my very first photograph of the Bypass Diner in Harrisburg, Pennsylvania. Now, over thirty years and 820 diners later, I believe I can say that this fascination has become more of an obsession. Back in those early days of documenting diners, I always planned to take my dad to a diner for breakfast but kept putting it off, thinking that he would be around for quite some time. Unfortunately, Dad passed on way too soon in 1982 at the young age of fifty-nine, so I never got my chance. But I take comfort in knowing that he was the one who started me on the road that has ultimately led to the publication of this book.

Whether you are a novice or true diner aficionado, *Classic Diners of Massachusetts* will introduce you to some of what I believe to be the classic diners currently operating in the Bay State. To make it easy, I will break it down by region. Each chapter will represent a region and will include a list of diners currently operating in that area, followed by "featured diners," the diners I personally believe to be the highlights of that particular region. To be sure, others may have a different list of favorites, and that's okay, as each diner generally has its own sort of character, ambiance and sometimes menu variations that make it unique.

For the novice, I will start your education by giving you what I consider the definition of a classic diner: a custom-built (prefabricated) building, built in one or more sections and delivered to a predetermined operating location that usually features an interior setup of a counter with stools, as well as booths and tables for seating. Diners historically have been constructed by a handful of manufacturers primarily located in the northeastern United States. In some cases, we will note that a few diners listed here were actually built on-site (non-factory-built) or located in existing buildings. Over the years, I have expanded the criteria for the definition to make exceptions for these, as they represent by their layout, ambience and menu served a great example of a true diner-like experience that should not be ignored.

DISCLAIMER: Due to the nature of the diner business in general, information contained here about any one particular diner as far as operating hours, ownership, menu, etc. is subject to change at any time. In most instances, I tried not to mention prices, as these are also subject to change. Also, as a side note, when looking over menu items for all the "Featured Diners," I noticed that the word "omelet" is spelled at least two different ways. I opted for the shorter spelling, just to keep things simple.

A Brief History and Timeline

In this day and age, there are still people who believe that all diners are converted trolley or train cars. While we cannot argue that over the years there were some diners converted from streetcars and railroad rolling stock, this was the exception rather than the rule. In fact, there are three examples in Massachusetts. The first example, Sisson's Diner in South Middleboro (currently closed), is a converted trolley car ironically built by Wason Manufacturing Company of Springfield, Massachusetts, which also built Brill Diners for the J.G. Brill Company of Philadelphia, Pennsylvania. The second example is the Club Car of Nantucket Island (open seasonally), which is a converted railroad car. Another railroad car converted to restaurant use is the Bagel Express Café in Somerset.

Diners actually have their own unique history that started here in New England in 1872, primarily in Providence, Rhode Island. Shortly thereafter, they were taken to a whole new level in Worcester, Massachusetts. In Massachusetts, there is a unique collection of diners, with the oldest dating from the early 1920s and the newest to the year 2000. Most of the diners are between fifty and seventy years old. Part of the reason for this was the demise of the local builder, the Worcester Lunch Car Company. Worcester built and delivered its last diner in 1957, and the assets of the company were auctioned off in 1961. As history has shown with the advent of split-construction (another term is modular construction), the mid-Atlantic diner manufacturers were continually building bigger and better diners or, as they were beginning to be called, diner-restaurants. The price of shipping these diners was starting to be restrictive, and after the late 1950s, only a handful were delivered to the Bay State and northern New England in general.

The number of diners in Massachusetts primarily seems to follow the demographics of the state, with there being more diners in eastern and central regions. Basically, the farther west you go from the coast, the number of diners dwindles, with the exception of Greater Worcester, which has a high concentration. It could also be said there were more diners in the mill cities than out in the rural areas, although this was mostly true thirty years ago; that number has decreased by the year 2011.

The following is a historic timeline of the evolution from lunch wagon to diner to large multi-sectioned restaurants. This information is based on the work originally researched and compiled by my colleague and friend Richard J.S. Gutman, who wrote the definitive history of diners in the book *American Diner Then & Now* (HarperCollins, 1993, and reprinted by Johns Hopkins University Press, 2000).

PROVIDENCE, RHODE ISLAND—1872: Walter Scott introduced the first night lunch wagon, a converted freight wagon with windows cut into the sides. Due to the fact that most restaurants closed after 8:00 p.m., Scott saw a ready-made clientele of night-shift workers and other people out and about in the late evening and into the overnight hours. He handed out previously prepared sandwiches, pie and coffee to these late-night customers who thronged his wagon. Within a short time, Scott had developed a fleet of these night lunches, and other businessmen saw the success that Scott was having and opened their own wagons. A standout among Scott's emulators, Ruel B. Jones, a Providence police patrolman, also became very successful running a fleet of seven wagons.

WORCESTER, MASSACHUSETTS–1884: Samuel Messer Jones, a cousin of Ruel Jones, moved to Worcester from Providence and introduced the first lunch wagon to this city. Sam Jones became successful enough by 1887 to afford to have a new wagon built, which was large enough to house a small kitchen and also to accommodate a handful of customers, who for the first time could actually come inside to order and eat their food. This feature was especially welcome on nights when the weather was inclement. In 1889, Jones sold all but one of his fleet of wagons to Charles H. Palmer.

Worcester, Massachusetts—1891: Charles Palmer received the first patent given for a lunch wagon design. This patent described what was to become the standard configuration for the next decade or so.

Worcester, Massachusetts—1892: Thomas H. Buckley started the New England Lunch Wagon Company, which later evolved into the T.H. Buckley Lunch Wagon and Catering Company. Not only did this company build lunch wagons, but it also sold equipment to be used in them. Buckley, who was described as the first "lunch wagon king," was credited with setting up wagons in some 275 towns across the country and was the originator of the White House Cafés, the fanciest and most famous of the mass-produced lunch wagons of the late 1890s.

Worcester, Massachusetts—1905: Wilfred H. Barriere, a carpenter who formerly worked for Buckley, went into business with blacksmith Stearns A. Haynes to form a new company constructing lunch wagons. This was taken over by Philip H. Duprey and renamed the Worcester Lunch Car and Carriage Manufacturing Company in 1906.

New Rochelle, New York—1905: Patrick J. Tierney began manufacturing lunch wagons and was credited with introducing many improvements to the lunch car during his tenure (1905–17).

Bayonne, New Jersey—1913: Jerry O'Mahony began manufacturing lunch cars with partner John J. Hanf. O'Mahony was destined to become the leading manufacturer of lunch wagons and diners for decades.

The above three manufacturers were the early pioneers in this industry, and many companies were to come after them. Many of these newer concerns were started from former employees of Tierney and O'Mahony, including, most notably, DeRaffele, Kullman and Fodero.

Haledon, New Jersey—1941: Paramount Diners patented the split construction method that became widely used by most companies thereafter. This enabled the manufacturers to build diners in multiple sections for transportation to operating locations. This method of modular construction continues to this day (2011), with a handful of companies still building what we term diners.

Chapter 1

Metropolitan Boston

From the first appearance of the horse-drawn lunch wagons in the late nineteenth century through the turn of the twentieth century, they were prevalent in business and recreational areas in Boston, as well as the surrounding communities. As time went on into the 1910s, some of these roving lunch wagons started interfering with traffic from other horse-drawn vehicles, as well as trolley cars and automobiles. Citing traffic and curfew laws, cities and towns started to curtail the hours of operation of these lunch wagons to the overnight hours, which severely limited the amount of money the lunch wagon proprietors could make.

Some of these enterprising souls saw that they could circumvent the traffic laws by setting their wagon on a sliver of land off-street and continue to operate at all hours. The lunch wagon manufacturers saw that the need for transporting them nightly was starting to change, so they started building the wagons longer and wider. This new larger configuration added more seating and kitchen space to the wagons. Also, at this point in time, eating in a railroad dining car was considered the height of luxury, and the longer lunch wagons were being designed with a strong resemblance to their railroad counterparts. So by the mid-1920s, the term "lunch wagon" had been supplanted by the term "dining car" or the shortened version—"diner." From that point on, diners started to become full-service restaurants serving breakfast, lunch and dinner.

At one time, there were countless diners in the metropolitan Boston area. From the 1920s through the late 1950s, they seemed to be everywhere! Diners even weathered the Depression of the 1930s fairly well. Production

In this postcard view circa 1910, we see a lunch wagon located on a plot of land adjacent to the sidewalk in downtown Mansfield. This wagon still has its wheels but is more than likely stationary, seeing that it has a canopy over the roof to deflect the hot summer sun and keep the inside of the wagon cooler. *Collection of the author.*

Here is another postcard view showing a lunch wagon just outside the entrance to the Columbia Dance Hall at Salisbury Beach. Enterprising lunch wagon operators learned early on that not only in-town business districts but town greens, parks and other recreational areas were prime locations to sell their food. *Collection of the author.*

halted during World War II but resumed with a vengeance after 1945, when construction supplies became available. Also, there were many servicemen returning from military duty who wanted to get into the business, and the diner manufacturers did their best to meet the demand. This demand resulted in even more new diners opening in the area. By the mid-1960s, with competition from fast-food restaurants and real estate sometimes becoming more valuable than the business (in this case, diners) that occupied the property, diners started to disappear from the urban landscape little by little. Also, the distance and costs associated with shipping new diners from the factories in New York and New Jersey contributed to the dwindling of diners in northern New England.

The diners that remain in this region seem to represent a little bit from almost every time period—diners from the late 1920s, like Buddy's Diner in Somerville, to the 1930 vintage ones like the Liberty Diner in Boston, as well as the Lunch Box Diner in Malden. There are diners from the 1940s, like the Rosebud Diner and Kelly's Diner, both in Somerville, and Wilson's Diner of Waltham. There are two late-model Worcester Lunch Cars: the Breakfast Club in Allston (1953), still operating, and the Lanna Thai Diner in Woburn (1952), which serves a nontraditional menu. There is even a 1965 vintage Swingle diner, Victoria's Diner in Boston. There are also quite a few on-site diners represented, in storefronts like Charlie's Sandwich Shoppe, Mul's Diner and Mike's City Diner in Boston, as well as the Arlington Diner-Restaurant in Arlington, Ernie's Lunch in Melrose and the Paul Revere Restaurant in Medford. On-site, stand-alone diners here are the South Street Diner in Boston and the Deluxe Town Diner in Watertown.

List of Diners in Region

Arlington Diner
134 Massachusetts Avenue, Arlington
On-site

Beachmont Roast Beef
619 Winthrop Avenue, Revere
Worcester Lunch Car Company (No. 811)

Breakfast Club
270 Western Avenue, Allston
Worcester Lunch Car Company (No. 841)

Broadway Diner
117 Broadway, Arlington
On-site (former Dairy Queen)

Buddy's Diner
113 Washington Street, Somerville
Worcester Lunch Car Company (No. 624)

Charlie's Sandwich Shoppe
429 Columbus Avenue, Boston
On-site

Deluxe Station Diner
70 Union Street, Newton
On-site (in Historic Railroad Station)

Deluxe Town Diner
627 Mount Auburn Street, Watertown
On-site/Worcester Lunch Car Company

The Diner at 11 North Beacon
11 North Beacon Street, Watertown
On-site

Drive-In Diner
419 Lee Burbank Highway (Route 1A), Revere
On-site

Ernie's Lunch
458 Franklin Street, Melrose
On-site

Johnny's Luncheonette
30 Langley Road, Newton
On-site

Kelly's Diner
674 Broadway, Somerville
Jerry O'Mahony Diners

Knotty Pine Restaurant
295 Auburn Street, Auburndale
On-site

Lanna Thai Diner
901 Main Street, Woburn
Worcester Lunch Car Company (No. 834)

Liberty Diner
1003 Massachusetts Avenue, Boston
Worcester Lunch Car Company
Lunch Box Diner
906 Eastern Avenue, Malden
Worcester Lunch Car Company (No. 690)

Mike's City Diner
1714 Washington Street, Boston
On-site

Mul's Diner
75 West Broadway, South Boston
On-site

New Yorker Diner
39 Mount Auburn Street, Watertown
On-site

Paul Revere Restaurant
447 High Street, Medford
On-site

Rosebud Diner
381 Summer Street, Somerville
Worcester Lunch Car Company (No. 773)

South Street Diner
178 Kneeland Street, Boston
On-site

Victoria's Diner
1024 Massachusetts Avenue, Boston
Swingle Diners

Wilson's Diner
507 Main Street, Waltham
Worcester Lunch Car Company (No. 819)

SOUTH STREET DINER, 178 KNEELAND STREET, BOSTON

1940s, built on-site

The South Street Diner is actually on Kneeland Street (at the corner of South Street). It began life as the Blue Diner and operated under that name for decades. The business started out in a small, barrel-roofed Worcester

The South Street Diner is Boston's only twenty-four-hour diner. Here we see it early on a Sunday about 4:00 a.m. This diner was built on-site and replaced a smaller barrel-roof Worcester lunch car.

Lunch Car probably dating from the 1930s. According to current owner Sol Sidell, around 1943 or so, the owners decided they wanted a larger building and had a new diner built on-site, replacing the original building. This newer diner is a brick structure that has dark blue lexan panels (these replaced vitrolite glass panels) around the windows and either ribbed stainless steel or aluminum sheeting covering the brickwork on the front and left side walls, as well as a metal sheathed roof. The interior is a very large and airy space, which reinforces its status as an on-site-built diner. In the mid- to late 1980s, the Blue Diner was taken over by Don Levy, who coined the term "Fine Dinering" to describe his vision for the revamped menu, which became slightly upscale. After a few years, Don "moved" the business and the name Blue Diner a couple of doors down to the former site of another restaurant he ran, previously called the Loading Zone, leaving the old Blue Diner empty. The former Blue Diner soon reopened as the Boston Diner for a brief time, and on March 4, 1997, it became the South Street Diner, helmed by the capable Sidell.

Sidell told me that ever since he was a young boy, it has always been his dream to run a restaurant where everyone felt comfortable. He went on to describe his route to owning and operating the South Street Diner. A Massachusetts native, Sidell is a seasoned and varied veteran in a multitude of capacities. Over time, he has climbed the ranks to the top of the restaurant and hospitality industry and has been fortunate enough to interlace his personal passion for charitable endeavors with a passion for his career. At age twelve, he was anxious to begin his livelihood, and at the suggestion of his mother, the Lynn native took a job at a local pizza parlor. Starting his path at the grass-roots level, he began by washing dishes in the kitchen. Within six months, the precocious Sidell was given his first promotion. While propped up on milk crates, he would toss pizzas in the windows, to the marvel of onlookers.

His passion realized, Sidell then took a series of culinary positions at restaurants throughout the North Shore, only breaking when school extracurricular activities interfered. Upon graduating from Lynn English High School, he set his heart on a degree in hotel restaurant management at Bunker Hill Community College. Wanting to whet his palate as an independent operator, Sidell purchased a hot dog stand and situated it outside top nightclubs and the Registry of Motor Vehicles to capitalize on the heavy foot traffic. Soon, the single hot dog stand became six, and Sidell took his entrepreneurship one step further by leasing a nightclub. With a burning desire to return to his culinary roots, he took a position at the Hyatt Regency, where he was trained in the art of fine dining. This took him one

Inside the South Street Diner as the late-night rush is winding down. Some cleanup is going on as the remaining patrons enjoy their food. There are almost as many servers and cooks as there are customers.

step further to the ubiquitous Palm Restaurant. From his humble roots and storied career in the restaurant and hospitality industry, Sidell's ownership in South Street Diner has been his lifelong dream, with the unwavering goal of exceeding customers' expectations, catering to all denominations of class and race and leaving a legacy of his passion.

Boston's only twenty-four-hour, seven-day licensed diner, Sidell says he is constantly updating and renovating South Street Diner with new equipment and new menu ideas. He recently installed new ceiling panels, as well as restrooms, and has also replaced the fixed counter stools with movable ones. He told me the old stools were being damaged by constant abuse by customers and the movable ones make it easier to clean the floor. Because the diner is open around the clock, the clientele can run from office workers and tourists to the fairly outrageous and unique, especially in the wee hours after all the nightclubs have closed.

The South Street Diner's offerings are varied, serving breakfast, lunch and dinner. Breakfasts include the usual eggs, omelets, pancakes and waffles, as well as breakfast sandwiches. There are seven different breakfast specials, including two sizes of steak and eggs (six ounce and one pound), as well as a

Monte Cristo with home fries and even something called Chocolate Fantasy French Toast. There is also a "Diner Special" that includes three eggs, two pancakes or French toast with home fries and your choice of meat—bacon, corned beef hash, ham or sausage.

The lunch and dinner menu features various appetizers, sandwiches, club sandwiches, salads, submarines and wraps, as well as burgers and grilled selections. Dinners are served with a choice of two sides—mashed potatoes, rice, French fries, salad or veggies—and the entrees are mixed grill (chicken, steak tips, grilled portobello, Italian sausages or grilled pork loin). You can choose one for ten dollars or two for fifteen dollars. There is also a one-pound New York sirloin served with two sides for fourteen dollars. They also have seasonal specials that run the gamut of lighter fare in the summer—salads and sandwiches—to heavier fare in the winter—meatloaf dinner and turkey dinners. These seasonal specials usually last for three months.

The South Street features its blue plate specials of the day and also likes to create a theme menu around all events and holidays, such as potato pancakes at Hanukkah, corned beef and cabbage for St. Patrick's Day, etc. It also runs complete meal specials such as the Bostonian clam chowder, lobster roll and French fries and either a Boston cream pie or a "locally grown apple" individual pie for fifteen dollars. Another special is the burger, beer and French fries for ten dollars. The South Street Diner now does all its own baking and serves twenty-two selections of beer, as well as four selections of mimosas and wine. It also has outdoor seating in the summer.

VICTORIA'S DINER, 1024 MASSACHUSETTS AVENUE, BOSTON

1965 Swingle Diner

I personally have witnessed a lot of the changes to Victoria's Diner over the years. My dad brought me to this diner when it was brand-new in 1965 (I was twelve years old at the time), and I have been patronizing it ever since. This 1965 version of Victoria's Diner is one of the newer diners in the Boston area, but is the last in a series of diners operated by the Georgenes family. The family, along with some friends, ran a chain of diners through the 1930s and 1940s in the Greater Boston area. Most of the diners were called the United Diners, but the flagship was the very large Old Colony Diner that was located on the corner of Old Colony Avenue and Dorchester Avenue

Victoria's Diner is currently the newest diner operating in Boston. Delivered circa 1965 from the Swingle Diner Company, this building has gone through some changes over the years, both inside and out.

in South Boston. The other diners were in Roxbury Crossing, Weymouth, Quincy and Somerville. As a side note, the Georgeneses were also related by marriage to two other Greek American families who had also started small diner chains in the area: the Galanis family, who had the Agawam Diners in Ipswich, Rowley and Peabody; and the Kallas family, who had both the Salem Diner in Salem and the Bel-Aire Diner in Peabody.

In the late 1940s, when the Old Colony/United Diners chain broke up, George Georgenes continued on with two of the diners, which he eventually sold. In 1949, he bought a brand-new stainless steel Jerry O'Mahony Diner from New Jersey and placed it on Massachusetts Avenue, a promising location on a highly traveled route. Even though this location was eventually bypassed by the Southeast Expressway, the business managed to survive with the help of the area's changing demographics, primarily the relocated meatpacking industry to the nearby New Market area and, more recently, by the new retail development of the South Bay Shopping Center in the next block. Operated by George's sons, Charles and Nicholas, since 1956, the diner thrived. By the mid-1960s, they were ready for a newer, larger diner. This would be the current Victoria, a large two-section colonial style with factory-built entry/vestibule manufactured by Swingle Diners. Over the years, the Georgenes family updated the diner and eventually added a

Since the newest operators took over the "Vic," the diner has had a resurgence in business. There is usually a wait to get a seat on a Sunday in the late morning and early afternoon.

back dining room in the 1970s, called the Café George after their dad. They also secured a piece of land across the street for an expanded parking lot in the 1980s, around the time they changed the name from Victoria Restaurant (they dropped the "Diner" from the name in the 1970s) to Victoria Dining.

By the end of 2003, both Charlie and Nick felt it was time to retire and ended up selling the business to Jay Hajj, a young chef/entrepreneur who was already running Mike's City Diner about a mile and a half away on Washington Street. Hajj spent some time updating the interior and reopened it as Victoria's Diner in 2004. Jay did a great job running both places for about three years but decided he was spreading himself too thin. He decided to lease the diner to George Athanasopoulas, another young chef/entrepreneur, who stepped in and took over the reigns on June 24, 2007. Athanasopoulas, who had already been running a late model Worcester Diner in the Allston section of Boston known as the Breakfast Club since April 2002, certainly had the right amount of experience to continue the Victoria's legacy.

Victoria's Diner is open seven days a week for breakfast, lunch and dinner (open twenty-four hours a day, Thursday, Friday and Saturday). The menu is extensive, featuring a little of everything. Breakfast is served all day, featuring all the typical egg dishes served with home fries or grits and your choice of toast. Pancakes, French toast and waffles are well represented, and there is even fresh baked banana bread that you can get grilled as a starter or as a French toast selection. There is a strawberry shortcake French toast, as well as Oreo-stuffed pancakes and Uncle Eddie's cakes, which are a stack of pancakes stuffed with sliced strawberries, bananas and blueberries. There are eighteen kinds of omelets, from the usual western and vegetarian to the international Italian, Greek, Florentine and Mediterranean to the more adventurous like ham and asparagus, lumberjack and New Market Omelet. Eggs Benedict comes nine different ways: the traditional, Blackstone, Florentine, Tuscan, corned beef hash, Empire, Atlantic, Roma and Savory, served with the Vic's homemade Benedict sauce, home fries or grits. You can even create your own Benedict and omelets with additions of different veggies, meats and cheeses. The Simply Plain Omelet starts at $5.69, and add-ons are $0.99 each. Breakfast sandwiches are popular, with everything from a breakfast burrito or breakfast taco to a breakfast burger or a western burger. Side orders are numerous, with an unusual amount of sausage items like turkey sausage and apple maple sausage, along with pork sausage, beef sausage, sausage patties, hot sausage and linguica.

Lunch features several panini-style sandwiches like the Pressed Pilgrim, Caprese, tuna melt and baked meatloaf, each served with French fries. There are even more signature sandwiches here, including Asiago chicken with bacon on ciabatta, a Grilled Rachael—which is fresh sliced turkey, coleslaw, Swiss cheese and Thousand Island dressing on grilled rye bread—as well as a Monte Cristo sandwich and a chicken cutlet sandwich. There are several half-pound burger selections to choose from, like a hickory BBQ burger, a blue cheese burger with sautéed onions and a Black-Jack Melt Burger. The Vic offers two quarter-pound all-beef Pearl brand hot dogs that can also be ordered as chili dogs for a little more. There are quite a few fresh salads featured, and all are served with pita bread and a large variety of dressings to choose from on the side.

The dinner menu is no less extensive, with appetizers, entrees, soups and side dishes. Victoria's special beer-battered onion rings, coconut shrimp and cheesy cheddar curly fries are standouts on the appetizer menu, as well as spinach and artichoke dip. Soups are represented by New England clam chowder, a Croc'O Chili or chicken lemon rice, all served by a cup or a bowl. Dinners are all mid-priced here (this being downtown Boston). Red meat selections range from steak and mashed potatoes to center cut pork chops to lightly seasoned steak tips. Tortilla-crusted tilapia, lemon butter shrimp and lemon butter broiled salmon are some of the fish selections, and chicken is represented by chicken broccoli penne, chicken Milanese and grilled chicken breast, among others. There is a veal dish—osso bucco, a braised veal shank that falls off the bone—and a traditional turkey dinner with all the trimmings. Shepherd's pie and boneless short ribs are also available. A large variety of side dishes are offered, like sweet potato fries, garlic mashed potatoes, coleslaw and rice pilaf. Healthy sides include a house or Caesar Salad, broccoli, butternut squash, grilled asparagus and sautéed spinach.

Desserts highlighted on the menu include a towering chocolate cake (a dessert for two—or one, if you dare), carrot cake, Boston cream cake or bourbon pecan pie. Various other pies are available, such as lemon meringue, chocolate cream, sky-high apple or blueberry and something called a Fruit of the Forest Pie (filling includes blueberries, blackberries, strawberries and raspberries). Other dessert items include old-fashioned bread pudding and Grapenut pudding.

The Vic also has a slightly different menu for the twenty-four-hour, early mornings/late nights crowd. The offerings are pared down from the regular menu, and the prices are slightly higher. Victoria's Diner has a full liquor license, serving a good selection of bottled beer, several examples of red and white wines and nine types of cordials, including Southern Comfort, Ouzo, Sambuca, Grand Marnier and five others. Victoria's serves cocktails like the usual Bloody Marys and margaritas to a little more unusual ones like the Green Monster, Tootsie Roll, Strawberry Creamsicle and Vic's Frozen Peach. It also has coffee drinks like Italian coffee (Sambuca and coffee topped with whipped cream), Vermont coffee (Cruzan dark rum, maple syrup and coffee with whipped cream) and Hot Almond (Disaronno Amaretto and coffee with whipped cream) plus two others.

Rosebud Diner, 381 Summer Street, Somerville

1941 Worcester Lunch Car

The Rosebud Diner is one place I can recall from a young age. But when I was young it was a bar, not serving food. The Nichols family has owned the diner since the late 1950s. When they first bought it, it was a regular working diner. But as the story goes, one day in 1957, the cooks came in and discovered that the cooking area had been dismantled and the diner was being turned into a cocktail bar and lounge and that they were basically out of a job. The diner continued to be used in this fashion and even acquired a mansard roof replacing a canvas awning across the front façade in the early 1970s.

The Rosebud Diner, as seen in this postcard view, is a classic example of a semi-streamlined Worcester lunch car, circa 1941. This diner operated for many years as a bar/cocktail lounge before being resurrected as a diner in the mid-1990s. In this photo, you can see the entrance to the Rosebud Bar & Grill in the rear, which was formerly known as the Surrey Room for many years. *Postcard photo by the author*.

In this view, we can see the Rosebud during its heyday as a cocktail lounge. A mansard hid the original monitor roof, as seen in this photo from the early 1980s. Also in the shot is the sign for the Surrey Disco behind the diner; that really helps date the photo.

The Nicholses sold the diner circa 1989 (if I remember correctly), and it continued to be used as a bar with limited food service under at least two operators until the mid-1990s, when the people who had bought the diner defaulted on the mortgage. The Nicholses stepped back in at this point and decided to give the place a limited restoration and operate it as a diner again. Bill Nichols said he was inspired by Dick Gutman's *American Diner Then & Now* history book. During the restoration, Bill even left a message on my answering machine to let me know that they had removed the mansard from the structure, exposing the original "monitor roof" of the diner. I had been after him to "take the mansard off" for years!

With the Rosebud's reopening, it has been reborn as slightly more upscale than the local neighborhood diner, offering breakfast, lunch and dinner, along with a full liquor license. Breakfast is served daily from 8:00 a.m. to 3:00 p.m. and features the usual eggs, pancakes, French toast and Belgian waffles. Breakfast specials include a Ham Quickie (scrambled eggs with diced ham), the Scrambler (scrambled eggs with choice of broccoli, spinach or asparagus topped with melted American cheese served over home fries) and homemade corned beef hash with two eggs. All egg dishes and specials are

When the Rosebud was brought back to being a diner, some minor restoration work was done on the interior. All the surviving original woodwork was refinished, and new ceiling panels and light fixtures were installed.

served with home fries and toast. There are Mega Omelets and International Mega Omelets, as well as eggs Benedict and eggs Rockefeller.

The lunch and dinner menu, which is offered daily until 11:00 p.m., is loaded with everything from soups and starters to salads, sandwiches, burgers and selections from the grill, as well as house specialties. The soups include French onion, homemade chili and New England clam chowder. The starters run the gamut from grilled veggies and artichoke hearts to flaming mushrooms, fried calamari and nachos grande. There are six different salads offered, including garden, Caesar, chicken Caesar and a grilled vegetable salad, along with Greek salad and grilled chicken salad. Featured sandwiches include a double-decker club, roast turkey, the Rosebud (a charbroiled chicken breast on a roll topped with cheddar cheese, red onion, lettuce, tomato and a tangy honey mustard), a fish sandwich called the Captain's Sandwich and the Dijon (thinly sliced imported ham and Swiss piled high with lettuce and tomato on a roll). All sandwiches are served with peddler fries or French fries, coleslaw or potato salad. The items from the grill are varied, with selections like grilled Italian sausage and grilled chicken breast to BBQ steak tips or lamb tips. Center cut pork chops, blackened or BBQ, are popular, along with pork chops and vinegar peppers and grilled swordfish or salmon.

House specialties include pasta and meatballs, meatloaf dinner and fish and chips, not to mention chicken broccoli and ziti, fettuccine primavera and even fettuccine puttanesca. Chicken parmigiana, roast turkey, mussels fra diavlo and sirloin shish-kabob or lamb shish-kabob round out this part of the menu. Ten different varieties of half-pound hamburgers are offered, including the Original Charburger, a BBQ burger, Cajun burger and a California veggie burger. There is also a dinner omelet available called the Rosebud Omelet. The Rosebud has a companion bar and grill around back, behind the diner, that features its own menu. One of the items is a great "bar pie" small pizza that I happen to like. The bar and grill, which opens at 5:00 p.m., has live music on occasion, and there are a couple of pool tables set up if you are so inclined.

BUDDY'S DINER, 113 WASHINGTON STREET, SOMERVILLE

1929 Worcester Lunch Car

Stepping inside Buddy's Diner is like going back in time. First of all, as most diners of this vintage, the front door slides open into a wall pocket. This is usually a little daunting for the uninitiated patron who tries to push or pull the door open until he realize his mistake or the customers already inside shout, "Slide it!" A very small diner, it has no booth service, just the counter and stools. There are also two shelf counters on either side of the front door with a handful of stools to accommodate seven or eight more patrons. A good portion of the cooking is done right behind the counter, in sight of the patron. There is also an attached building to the rear with a kitchen for more prep and cooking. This diner started out a good forty miles to the west in Leominster and was known as Sawin's Diner when it was delivered there in 1929 from Worcester. It reportedly was moved to its current location in the early 1950s, when it was operated as Cousin's Diner by Max Strebnick and a few years later as Jerry's Diner by Jerry Ludy. It was during this period right after it got to Somerville that the exterior painted metal panels were exchanged for sunburst-style stainless steel panels. It became Buddy's Truck Stop circa 1965, when Buddy Barrett took over the operation. Barrett was a longtime diner man who had operated or worked in various diners in places such as Revere and Saugus.

In the early 1980s, the original windows were replaced by newer models, and the wooden molding at the edge of the roof was changed as

This exterior photo of Buddy's Diner shows the "sunburst" stainless steel panels that were installed on the diner after it came to Somerville. The windows were updated in the early 1980s. Some new customers still try to open the front door by either pulling or pushing it. When this happens, the people on the inside shout, "Slide it!"

The inside of Buddy's shows all the seating is at the counter or the shelves at the front wall on stools. This is typical of 1920s vintage diners.

well. The Barrett family continued to operate Buddy's until 2006, when Buddy's son John (and John's wife, Sue) decided to retire and move to Georgia. John sold the diner to Somerville native Nicole Bairos, who changed the name to Buddy's Diner—but the name is pretty much all she changed. Although the diner is currently owned by Nicole Bairos, she has apparently turned over the daily operation of the place to her cousins Kim Bairos and Niko Makrigiannis, along with short-order cook extraordinaire José Ramirez. The menu has largely stayed the same, with all the basics. Breakfast is big at this small diner—eggs any style, home fried potatoes and toast, along with the usual sides of bacon, ham or sausage. Italian sausage is also available, along with real, homemade corned beef hash and even fried baloney. French toast and pancakes also are favorite breakfast options at Buddy's. Daily lunch specials include turkey dinner on Tuesdays, roast beef on Wednesdays, roast pork on Thursdays and haddock and baked macaroni and cheese on Fridays. Meatloaf is available Tuesday through Friday. The diner is open for breakfast only on Mondays, with simple sandwiches like a BLT, hot dog, steak and cheese submarines and hamburgers.

KELLY'S DINER, BROADWAY, SOMERVILLE

1947 Jerry O'Mahony Diner

Larry Holmes, a longtime resident of Winthrop, Massachusetts, could be termed a renaissance man or, at the very least, an entrepreneur. Holmes has had a varied career, from running a Pepperidge Farm delivery route to owning a neighborhood bar and grill in Somerville (the city he grew up in), as well as owning and operating a couple of other restaurants in Winthrop. He even had a short stint as interim town manager while serving as the veterans' agent of that town. But I believe his most unique accomplishment was bringing two vintage diners to Massachusetts in the last twenty years and actually opening and operating them. Kelly's Diner is the second of the two. Holmes's dream of getting into the diner business goes back to the late 1980s, when he had a chance to buy a closed, 1930 vintage Worcester Lunch Car. This diner had been taken back in trade and refurbished by the same

Kelly's Diner shows a lot of stainless steel and flex glass stripes under the windows, as well as stainless steel trim above. The white band at the roofline was originally porcelain enamel in a cream color that has since been covered over. Jerry O'Mahony used this porcelain on the exterior of diners right after World War II, when stainless steel was hard to obtain. The fact that this diner shows the use of both materials means it was probably built in late 1947 or 1948.

This is a 1982 photo of Kelly's Diner at its original location in Delaware. Known as the Grecian Diner at that point, it started out life as part of a chain of Hollywood Diners.

company in the 1950s and had been operating in the town of Buzzard's Bay on Cape Cod since then under various names. After the purchase, Holmes had the diner transported to a storage yard near Boston, where it sat for a year or two while he attempted to find a location to set the diner back up in business. Those plans never were realized, and he eventually sold the diner. He revisited the dream of diner ownership again in 1992, when he purchased the former Peter Pan Diner of Kuhnsville, Pennsylvania, and moved it to Falmouth, Massachusetts (see Betsy's Diner in Chapter 3). After successfully setting up that diner in business and operating it for a couple of years, he sold it and moved on. This brings us to 1995 and the diner that is now called Kelly's Diner.

Kelly's Diner was built right after World War II, when the O'Mahony Company was starting to roll out diners again from its factory in Elizabeth, New Jersey. With the shortages brought on by the war effort, metal was still hard to get. So many of the diners produced right after the war by this company had porcelain steel panels for exterior covering instead of the harder to get stainless steel. Kelly's was a transitional model that still had the porcelain panels above the windows but stainless steel and flex-glass stripes below. This would date it to about 1947. Kelly's started out life on Route 13 in Hares Corner, Delaware. I found out recently that it was originally part of the Hollywood Diner chain based in Delaware. When I first came across this diner in 1982, it was still at its original location but operating under the name Grecian Diner. Between the time I found it in '82 and the mid-1990s, it traded under names such as Scotty's Diner and Frank's Diner. As fate would have it, the diner ultimately ended up being transported from Delaware to Somerville, about two and a half miles from where I was living in Medford circa 1995, when Larry Holmes purchased it.

Just prior to Holmes's purchase of Frank's Diner, there had been a small commercial building on the corner of Rogers Avenue and Broadway in the Ball Square neighborhood of Somerville. I believe this building housed a restaurant or store that had a devastating fire and facilitated the structure's demolition. Holmes saw an empty lot with much potential and moved fast to cut through a lot of red tape and obtain permits and approvals to locate a classic diner on the property. He then contacted Richard Gutman and asked him if he knew of any diners that might be available. Gutman suggested Frank's Diner. Holmes made a number of trips down to Delaware to inspect the diner and, most importantly, to take measurements. Holmes found out that the diner was going to be a tight fit but managed to squeeze it into the empty lot with six inches to spare. After the diner was installed, to look at it you would think it had always been there.

The diner came into Somerville in December of that year on two flatbed trailers. Because there were obstructions on the sidewalk—electrical utility boxes, traffic lights and streetlights, etc.—it was determined that the diner had to be placed on the foundation coming from the rear. This means the front section was placed on the foundation first and the rear section last. The diner was then worked on to bring it up to modern codes (plumbing and electrical), with modifications for handicapped access. It finally opened in September 1996. Holmes named the diner after his daughter, Kelly August, who, along with her brother Jay Holmes, currently operates the business with a seasoned crew of cooks and waitresses.

Kelly's offers the usual breakfast selections—eggs, three-egg omelets (all eggs and omelets are served with toast and home fries), breakfast sandwiches and bagels, along with pancakes and French toast. There are assorted homemade muffins, along with other side dishes. A six-ounce sirloin steak and eggs special is popular, as is linguica and eggs. Portions are large! Lunch includes a selection of deli-style sandwiches, burgers and three-decker club sandwiches. There are soups, stews and chowders, made fresh daily. There is even a soup

Kelly's Diner is very popular during the week but gets really jammed on Saturdays and Sundays. The interior is very original, with slight modifications to bring it up to handicapped-accessibility codes.

and half-sandwich option. There are several lunch platters and salad plates, as well as a children's menu. Operating hours are Monday through Saturday, 6:00 a.m. to 3:00 p.m., and Sundays, 6:00 a.m. to 2:00 p.m. (breakfast only).

DELUXE TOWN DINER, 627 MOUNT AUBURN STREET, WATERTOWN

1947, built on-site

The diner currently known as the Deluxe Town Diner started out life as the Town Diner, a monitor roof–style Worcester Lunch Car built in the late 1920s or early 1930s. It got an extreme makeover in 1947, when the Contos family decided they wanted a larger, more modern diner. Instead of, say, going back to the Worcester Lunch Car Company to build them a new diner, they hired a local contractor who was sensitive to the styles of diners being produced at the time. They wrapped the original diner with a very large building, making the old diner the kitchen for the new establishment.

When I first started frequenting this diner in the early 1980s, it was still being run by George Contos and his brother-in-law, Chris Morris. One day, Chris handed me a circa 1960 menu to look at while I sat at the counter. The highest-priced items on the menu were $1.50. One item was an open lobster salad sandwich served with tartar sauce, golden brown French fried potatoes, coleslaw with roll and butter. Another was an open sirloin steak sandwich served with French fried potatoes, tossed salad, roll and butter. You would be hard pressed to get either of these dishes today for under $10.00 anywhere! George and Chris retired about 1983 or '84 and sold the diner to Arthur and Angela Arvanitis, who operated the diner until the year 2000, when they leased the business, turning over the operation to Don and Daryl Levy. The Levys took a short period of time to give the place a thorough cleaning and updating. Reopening it as the Deluxe Town Diner, Don and Daryl brought their "Fine Dinering" concept that had worked well for them at Boston's Blue Diner in the late 1980s to Watertown and have not looked back. To be sure, the menu is slightly more upscale, along with the prices, compared to your run-of-the-mill diner.

The Deluxe Town Diner still looks good after sixty-plus years of service. With its glass block rounded corner windows, two-tone porcelain-enameled panels and streamlined roof, not to mention its neon sign, this place is still a head-turner.

Showing a lot of ceramic tile, stainless steel and leatherette, walking into the Deluxe Town Diner is like stepping back in time. This diner was brought back to life when Don and Daryl Levy took over the operation in the late 1990s.

Serving breakfast all day, 7:00 a.m. to 10:00 p.m., seven days a week, the menu items at first glance seem typical until you look a little closer. Sure, there are fried eggs and omelets, as well as breakfast sandwiches, wraps and burritos with all the sides of bacon, sausage, ham and corned beef hash. But then you also can choose from deluxe specials like a Middle Eastern platter featuring hummus, tabouleh, falafel, feta cheese, Greek yogurt, hard boiled egg, olives and fresh pita bread. Another deluxe special is the smoked salmon platter featuring pastrami-style smoked salmon with cream cheese, sliced tomato, sweet onion, lemon and capers with a choice of toasted bagel. From the griddle you have a choice of deluxe sour cream flapjacks, ployes (a buckwheat and wheat flour pancake from a French Acadian recipe), New York potato pancakes, sweet potato pancakes, blue cornmeal pancakes and Rhode Island Johnnycakes. French toast made with challah bread is popular, and there are cheese blintzes too. There are brunch specials featured on Saturdays, Sundays and holidays (7:00 a.m. to 4:00 p.m.).

The lunch and dinner menu is also extensive, starting with soups and appetizers. Lunch features various sandwiches, club sandwiches and wraps, along with blue plate specials like meatloaf and roast turkey dinners, franks and beans, mac and cheese, chicken potpie and various burger and hot dogs. There are nine different types of fresh salads on the menu. For dinner choices, blue plates feature various meat, seafood and poultry dishes, along with dishes like a southern fried catfish po'boy, chicken picatta, east India curry chicken, Don's mother's chicken livers, calves liver and bacon, pot roast, chicken parm and even a vegetarian section that has vegan burgers, a four-vegetable plate, a couple of different veggie wraps and eggplant French fries, as well as eggplant meatballs. A kids' menu is available also. Beverages include at least twenty different types of fresh brewed teas, as well as the usual bottomless cup of coffee. But there are also choices of espresso, cappuccino, café au lait and café latte, among others. Frappes (milk shakes with ice cream), milkshakes or soy shakes, milk or soymilk and Dr. Brown's sodas, as well as other fountain drinks, are on the menu. Fourteen different bottled beers are available, along with white and red wines and mimosas. Desserts include pies, cakes, ice cream and puddings, as well as deluxe cupcakes.

As of early 2011, residents of the nearby city of Newton and the towns to the west do not have to drive the three or four miles into Watertown to partake of this uniquely extensive menu. Don and Daryl Levy recently opened a new restaurant called the Deluxe Station Diner housed in the historical H.H. Richardson–designed Newton Centre Train Station, located at 70 Union Street. It serves the same food and drinks as the Deluxe Town Diner.

Chapter 2

North Shore and Northern Suburbs

This region of Massachusetts historically had a high concentration of diners primarily because of the mill/factory cities of Lynn, Peabody, Salem, Haverhill, Lawrence and Lowell, as well as the port city of Gloucester. There were numerous lunch wagons from the late nineteenth century into the early twentieth century. These were eventually supplanted by the larger diners from the 1920s through the 1950s. By the 1960s, the number of these places started to dwindle along with the decline in manufacturing. By the early 1980s, when I started to document them, the major portion of diners only existed in the old manufacturing cities. Lynn still had four diners, Lowell had seven, Lawrence had three and Haverhill had only one. Peabody, until recently, held on to three (now only one is operating), and Salem, which had three diners circa 1980, now holds on to two. I cannot discount that all the major roads heading north from metro Boston through this region also had their share of diners, including U.S. Route 1. Roads like Route 1A, Route 28 and U.S. Route 3 (now State Route 3A) were also magnets for diners, but this has declined due to the opening of the interstate highways that bypassed the old roads. So now, most of the diners that are left here in this region of the Bay State date from the late 1920s to the early 1950s. There are some on-site and storefront-type diners in and around the North Shore and the northern suburbs that do well, including Rosie's Diner in North Chelmsford, the Dream Diner in Tyngsboro and the Shawsheen Luncheonette in Andover, as well as the North Avenue Diner in Wakefield and the Groveland Diner in Groveland. There are diners here that serve nontraditional menus, like the Golden Lake Restaurant in Lynn (formerly the Lynway Diner and Lynn Diner), Supreme Roast Beef in Gloucester (formerly the Cape Ann Diner) and the Trolley Pizzaria in Lowell (formerly Bryer's Streamliner Diner and Gorham Street Diner, among other names).

LIST OF DINERS IN REGION

Agawam Diner
166 Newburyport Turnpike (U.S. Route 1), Rowley
Fodero Dining Car Company

Cameo Diner
715 Lakeview Avenue, Lowell
On-site (evolved from lunch wagon)

Capitol Diner
431 Union Street, Lynn
Brill Dining Car

Charlie's Diner
297 South Broadway, Lawrence
Worcester Lunch Car Company (No. 720)

Club Diner
145 Dutton Street, Lowell
Worcester Lunch Car Company (No. 703)

Deb's (Pilgrim) Diner
4 Boston Street, Salem
Worcester Lunch Car Company. (No. 725)

Dream Diner
384 Middlesex Road, Tyngsboro
On-site

Fish Tale Diner
420 Bridge Road, at Bridge Marina, Salisbury
Worcester Lunch Car Company (No. 762)

Four Sisters Owl Diner
244 Appleton Street, Lowell
Worcester Lunch Car Company (No. 759)

Golden Lake Restaurant
38 Bennett Street, Lynn
Worcester Lunch Car Company (No. 833)

Groveland Diner
1 Elm Park, Groveland
On-site

Little Depot Diner
1 Railroad Avenue, Peabody
Worcester Lunch Car Company (No. 650)

North Avenue Diner
247 North Avenue, Wakefield
On-site

Paradise Diner
122 Bridge Street, Lowell
Worcester Lunch Car Company (No. 727)

Pat's Diner
11 Bridge Road, Salisbury
Worcester Lunch Car Company (No. 824)

Portside Diner
2 River Street, Danvers
Worcester Lunch Car Company (No. 813)

Rosie's Diner
27 Vinal Square, North Chelmsford
On-site

Salem Diner
70 Loring Avenue, Salem
Sterling Diners

Shawsheen Luncheonette
3 Lowell Street, Andover
On-site

Sunrise Diner
639 Broadway, Lawrence
On-site/possible Worcester Lunch Car

Supreme Roast Beef
218 Main Street, Gloucester
Jerry O'Mahony Diners

Three Dogz Diner
13 South Broadway, Lawrence
Worcester Lunch Car Company (No.750)

Trolley Pizzaria
984 Gorham Street, Lowell
Donald Evans–built streamlined diner

Tumble Inn Diner
488 Lincoln Avenue, Saugus
On-site

CAPITOL DINER, 431 UNION STREET, LYNN

1928 Brill Dining Car

The Capitol Diner is quite possibly one of the last operating Brill diners in the country. At one time, there were countless Brill diners operating around the Northeast and all the way to California. But as years have gone by, these numbers have dwindled substantially. The Capitol is located at its only operating location since it was delivered in 1928. The J.G. Brill Company headquartered in Philadelphia was well known most notably for its line of trolley cars and train trucks (the wheel assemblies for railroad cars). It branched out into diner manufacturing in the late 1920s. The following is excerpted from a short history on the back of the Capitol Diner's menu:

The Capitol Diner was built by Wason Manufacturing Company of Springfield, Mass., a subsidiary of the Brill Company in 1928. Bought brand-new by Ernest A. Goodwin in that year, it operated as the Miss Lynn Diner until 1938 when it was purchased by George Fennell, with the help of his brother Frank who renamed the diner after their neighbor across the street…E.M. Lowe's Capitol Theater. In 1948 George's nephew, Buddy Fennell, traveled from Saint John, New Brunswick, Canada by train to visit with his uncle and to look for job opportunities. Legend has it that Buddy arrived at the diner with suitcase in hand and said "Here I am Uncle George!" George replied with his diner sarcasm, "That's great—put on an apron and get behind the counter, I'm short-handed!" The rest is history. Buddy agreed to stay for six months to help his uncle. Fifty three years later, Buddy was not only still there, but became the owner of the business.

The Capitol Diner suffered damage to its interior due to a fire in the late 1970s but was brought back to a reasonable appearance, close to what it had been originally, and reopened within a few months. In the early

The Capitol Diner, with owner Bob Fennell standing proudly in front of this rare survivor. At one time, there were many of these Brill Steel Diners throughout the northeast. The Capitol is quite possibly the last one of its kind still in operation.

After a circa 1980 fire and a 1990s expansion, the interior of the Capitol Diner still looks great and features the original stools, as well as glass-topped counter.

1990s, new construction opened up the back wall of the diner and created a larger cooking area behind the counter, expanding into the former alley that existed between the diner and an adjacent building. Today, the Capitol Diner is helmed by Buddy's son Bob, who—along with an able staff that includes Bob's daughters Ashley and Tanya (working part time, weekends)—continues the tradition of offering the freshest quality food at reasonable prices. As in most Bay State diners, the Capitol is only open for breakfast and lunch. For breakfast, a customer can get the extra-large Grade A eggs three different ways: one extra-large egg, two extra-large eggs or three extra-large eggs cooked any style with the usual sides of bacon, sausage, hash or ham and, of course, home fried potatoes and toast. Pancakes and French toast are also available, along with breakfast sandwiches and even a breakfast burrito. There are also three extra-large egg omelets on the regular menu, along with unique breakfast specials served only on weekends. These usually change week to week, with selections that feature eggs Benedict and a couple of variations called Irish Benedict and Florentine Benedict (instead of Canadian bacon on the traditional eggs Benedict, the Irish Benedict has grilled sausage patties with sautéed mushrooms, and the Florentine features grilled sliced tomato and sautéed baby spinach). The weekend specials also include linguica and eggs, Portuguese sweet bread French toast and even a Philly cheese omelet, among others. Lunches include sandwiches, club sandwiches, burgers, specialty wraps, salad platters and quesadillas. Homemade soups, stews and chili are also available, along with garden salad and Caesar salad. The Capitol Diner recently has started offering breakfast anytime. Operating hours are Monday through Saturday, 6:00 a.m. to 2:00 p.m., and Sunday, 7:00 a.m. to 1:00 p.m.

Salem Diner, 70 Loring Avenue, Salem

1941 Sterling Diner

Currently, the Salem Diner is one of only two operating Sterling Streamliners (Sterling No. 4106). The other is the Modern Diner of Pawtucket, Rhode Island. To be sure, there are at least four others still in existence, but these are all in storage, and it is anyone's guess whether they will ever be put back into service. In fact, the Salem Diner is the only streamliner doing

Still at its original business location, the Salem Diner has the distinction of being one of two Sterling Streamliners still in operation. The other is the Modern Diner of Pawtucket, Rhode Island.

The interior of the Salem Diner was updated with new floor tile, as well as tile on the counter apron, when George and Zoe Elefteriadis took over the reins of this 1941 classic streamliner.

business at its original operating location. The first owner was a man named Frederick J. "Ted" Doherty, who sold the diner to brothers Jim and Bill Kallas in 1946. Bill Kallas left the Salem Diner in 1952 to join another brother, Peter, to start up and operate the Bel-Aire Diner on U.S. Route 1 in Peabody. Jim continued at the Salem and was joined by his son John. John took over the reins along with his cousin Ted Tsoutsouras in 1982. John had sold his interest in the business by 1989. Ted Tsoutsouras and his son Peter owned the diner until 2000, when they handed it off to Stella Georgakakis, who continued to operate it until 2007. Enter George and Zoe Elefteriadis, veteran owners of other restaurants in the Greater Boston area who came in and did a thorough cleaning and updating of the diner. They held a grand reopening in January 2008 with Boston Red Sox icon Johnny Pesky cutting the ceremonial ribbon. Pesky (a former teammate of Ted Williams and Dom DiMaggio), who is currently in his nineties, is a regular customer of the diner and was happy to do the honors for the special occasion.

George and Zoe retained most of the diner's employees from the previous ownership, and this helped keep things running smoothly in the transition. The staff at the Salem Diner is experienced and friendly, and service is quick.

The menu here is quite extensive for such a small diner serving only breakfast and lunch. Huge breakfast plates (plates include home fries and toast) are served, along with three-egg omelets, pancakes and French toast. There are also two-egg roll-ups and breakfast sandwiches available, as well as a selection of fresh baked muffins. The usual side dishes, like bacon, ham and sausage, are joined by Canadian bacon, Greek loukaniko and Italian sausage.

The Salem Diner features daily homemade lunch specials with soup and salad, with items ranging from chicken cacciatore, beef stroganoff and spaghetti and meatballs to stuffed peppers, roast lamb or pork and New England boiled dinner, to name just a few. Hot submarine sandwiches are represented by eggplant parmesan, chicken parmesan, Italian sausage with pepper and onions and even a Steak Bomb, with ten more items to choose from. Cold and hot sandwiches, along with pita wraps and club sandwiches, are offered with side dishes, including spinach pie, rice pilaf, French fries and onion rings.

There are also a half dozen dinner plates served with mashed potatoes or rice and vegetables with bread, along with Greek-influenced selections represented by what they refer to as select plates. These include beef or chicken kabob, spinach pie, Greek loukaniko and gyros that come with rice and Greek salad with Syrian bread. Deep-fried plates include chicken fingers, wing dings and fried chicken, along with fried filet of sole and fried haddock served with French fries and coleslaw. There are over half a dozen salad plates to choose from, as well as many different soups and chowders. Desserts include cheesecake, baklava and chocolate and carrot cake, along with various pies and puddings.

Operating hours are Monday through Saturday, 6:00 a.m. to 3:00 p.m., and Sundays (breakfast only) 7:00 a.m. to 2:00 p.m.

Little Depot Diner, 1 Railroad Avenue, Peabody

1929 Worcester Lunch Car

The Little Depot Diner is Worcester Lunch Car No. 650. It started life in 1929 as Harry's Diner in Lynn and also spent some time in Danvers as Cal's Diner prior to being moved to its current location in 1950 (according to Gary Thomas's *Diners of the North Shore*). Since it has been in Peabody, this small thirteen-stool diner operated under the name Holly's Diner for a time before being renamed Kurly's Diner by former owner Max Kurland. By the 1980s, when I first started going there, the diner remained almost 100 percent

Peabody's Little Depot Diner is one of the smallest diners in the state. The exterior features newer windows and T-111 wooden paneling that were installed in the 1980s. The current owners, Jim and Judy Miles, added an expanded entryway at the side entrance, as well as a porch on the kitchen annex. The Miles family has managed to bring this diner back to life after many years of being marginal, at best, under previous ownership.

The interior of the Little Depot Diner still features original tile work on the floor, counter apron and walls, along with original stools. Although the original marble countertop is still there, it was unfortunately covered over years ago with a plastic laminate. It does not take many people to pack this place, so all the customers are encouraged to basically "chew and screw" (not in those words, of course).

original inside and out. The Kurlands sold the diner I estimate by 1982 or '83, and at that point, the diner's back bar area was completely gutted. Even the nickel-plated copper hood was trashed. The original windows were changed, and the marble countertop was covered in Formica laminate. I was driving by one Saturday afternoon when this renovation was happening, and I saw that there was a dumpster full of pieces of the diner. I stopped and looked inside. I saw that there were original window frames in among the debris, and I pulled one out. I found the car number (650) stamped into the frame (something Worcester Lunch Car did back in the 1920s and '30s).

The only remaining original surfaces left after this were the tile walls, counter apron, wooden ceiling and ceramic tile floor. The name was changed to the Railroad Diner after the renovations were complete and was operated until the late 1990s by the late Marianna Cox. In January 2002, the diner was reopened by Barbara Henry, who christened it the Whistlestop Diner. Henry ran it for the next few years, and in 2008, Jim and Judy Miles did their magic to the interior of the old diner and, in keeping with the railroad theme started by Cox and continued by Henry, reopened it as the Little Depot Diner. Under the Mileses' stewardship, this place is now flourishing more than it has in quite some time. It was even featured on Guy Fieri's *Diners, Drive-Ins and Dives* TV show on the Food Network. On any weekend morning the place gets packed, although this is not hard to do considering the size and number of seats. But certainly it is also due to the quality of food being cooked in the kitchen.

Touted by the Miles family as "Home of the Honest Cup of Coffee," the diner is only open for breakfast and lunch Tuesday through Friday, 7:00 a.m. to 1:30 p.m. and Saturday and Sunday for breakfast only, 7:00 a.m. to 12:00 p.m. Breakfast selections include eggs any style, served with toast and home fries or Little Depot baked beans. Side orders of meat are extra. They also serve three-egg omelets, breakfast sandwiches and pancakes served with their "Special Butter" (maple caramel cinnamon butter). The three breakfast specials are the All Aboard! (the Little Depot's version of the hungry man's special), which is two eggs, two strips of bacon, two sausages and two pancakes with home fries or baked beans; the Train Wreck, which is two eggs dropped (New England term for poached) on hash with home fries, baked beans and brown bread or toast; and Hungry Hobo Hash, which is two eggs, corned beef hash and toast. Lunch selections feature simple sandwiches such as all-white-meat tuna, tuna melt, BLT and Angus beef hamburgers, cheeseburgers and bacon burgers, as well as grilled cheese (plain or with tomato or tomato and bacon), hot dogs and a ham and cheese club. These are served with your choice of home fries, baked beans, coleslaw or potato chips. Homemade soup is also available Tuesday through Friday. There are items you rarely see on any diner menu here as well, including a Fluffernutter sandwich and corton (Kuh-Toh-n), a French Canadian pork spread.

PORTSIDE DINER, 2 RIVER STREET, DANVERS

1948 Worcester Lunch Car

The Portside Diner, Worcester Lunch Car No. 813, originally known as the Cape Ann Grill, was delivered to its first operating location at 214 Main Street in Gloucester on June 8, 1948. It replaced a smaller diner, WLC No. 800, which had been delivered the previous year. Apparently, the original owners, Augustus Mulrenin and Henry Schluter, had done very well with the first diner and felt that they needed a larger one to handle the crowds. The smaller Cape

Although the porcelain-enameled panels on Danvers's Portside Diner still have the "Cape Ann" name emblazoned across the front, this is merely a nod to its past life in Gloucester, where it originally operated. The Worcester Lunch Car Company only built two diners of this size and layout, both in 1948. The other one was the Star Lite Diner of Medford, which has since been demolished.

The Portside Diner's interior is fairly intact. The original Formica ceiling was replaced after it was damaged in a fire. The back bar has also been altered by removing all the cooking equipment to the rear kitchen and cutting a new door across from the break in the counter to access the kitchen.

Ann was sold as a used diner to Arvo Niemi of Westminster, Massachusetts, who moved it adjacent to a gas station he owned on state Route 2 (now Route 2A) in Westminster. Niemi never changed the name of the diner because, as the story goes, the diner was still basically brand-new and it would have cost more money to have new porcelain panels fabricated, so it stayed the Cape Ann Diner, albeit fifty miles from the ocean. Meanwhile, Messrs. Mulrenin and Schluter had the new, larger Cape Ann installed back in Gloucester, but for some reason, this diner never met with the success of its earlier incarnation and was closed by 1951. According to Gary Thomas, author of *Diners of the North Shore*, the Cape Ann Grill was bought by Roland Michel in 1952, and he operated it for the next seven years. In 1959, Roland sold it with the stipulation that it needed to be moved no closer than twenty miles to his new diner in Gloucester. That was when the Cape Ann came to the Danversport neighborhood in Danvers and was renamed the Portside Diner.

Since then, the diner has been operated by a handful of people, most notably for the last twenty-five-plus years by the Andromidas family of Danvers, who have kept the diner open seven days a week, serving typical diner meals of breakfast, lunch and dinner at reasonable prices. James and Ekaterina "Kathy" Andromidas run the diner along with their three children—John Andromidas, Nikki Gkiokas and Peggy Giannarakis. The Andromidases keep long hours for this neck of the woods, operating Monday through Saturday, 6:00 a.m. to 8:00 p.m., and Sundays, 6:00 a.m. to 12:00 p.m. The only North Shore diner that keeps longer hours is the Agawam in Rowley. Meals at the Portside are reasonably priced, with the regular breakfast selections of eggs, omelets and breakfast sandwiches, along with French toast, pancakes and side orders of bacon, ham, sausage and hash. They also offer Greek sausage or kielbasa. The lunch and dinner menu features salads (seven kinds), sandwiches, club sandwiches and soups and chowder. Fried seafood is available also, as well as dinner plates. There are three specials every day of the week except Sunday (breakfast only). Desserts consist of blueberry or apple pie, something called John's Chocolate Tower and three types of pudding: Grapenut, bread and chocolate.

AGAWAM DINER, 166 NEWBURYPORT TURNPIKE (CORNER OF U.S. ROUTE 1 AND ROUTE 133), ROWLEY

1954 Fodero Diner

Everyone seems to know the Agawam, possibly one of the more popular diners in Massachusetts! Operated by the Galanis family since day one, this is the last of four diners that have carried the Agawam name. The Agawam Diner saga started out at Depot Square in downtown Ipswich with a small barrel-roofed Worcester Lunch Car in 1940 (Agawam #1). This first diner was replaced in 1947 by a larger Worcester Lunch Car, a semi-streamlined model (Agawam #2). At this point, Agawam #1 was sold to a family in Brunswick, Maine, but only stayed at its Cooks Corner location in Brunswick until 1950, when that owner could not make a go of the business. The Galanis family got the diner back and sent it to the Worcester Lunch Car Company for a refurbishing before having the building relocated to the present site at the corner of State Route 133 and U.S. Route 1 in Rowley.

In 1954, the Galanis family bought two modern stainless steel diners from the Fodero Dining Car Company of New Jersey. The larger of the two (Agawam #3) was brought to a location on U.S. Route 1 northbound at the Peabody/Lynnfield town line (where the Holiday Inn is currently located) in March of that year. The next November, the second Fodero (Agawam #4),

The Agawam Diner in Rowley is a familiar site to anyone traveling to and from New Hampshire on U.S. Route 1. The Galanis family has operated this place from day one and has lovingly kept the fifty-seven-year-old diner in close to factory condition. I lucked out when I stopped to snap this photo, as usually the front is blocked by patrons' cars.

This diner has operated in three different locations. This is a postcard image of the diner at its first location in Ipswich. After it left Ipswich, it operated for a number of years on U.S. Route 1 south in Peabody before moving to the Rowley location, circa 1970.

which was slightly smaller than Agawam #3, was delivered to Depot Square in Ipswich, where it replaced Agawam #2. Agawam #2 was sold and moved to Salem, where it operated as the Front Street Diner and later as the North Shore Diner. So at that point in time, the Galanises had three Agawam Diners operating simultaneously. This lasted until 1960, when Agawam #3 was forced off its site by eminent domain due to a highway interchange. Eventually, the diner was sold and became the Thunderbird Diner in Saugus (also on Route 1 northbound). Agawam #4 was moved in 1963 to Route 1 south in West Peabody, where it remained until 1970, when it came up to Rowley to replace Agawam #1. Agawam #1 was then sold and moved to Salisbury and is currently operating as the Fish Tale Diner. Whew! Glad I could get that straight!

The Agawam is open fairly long hours, serving breakfast, lunch and dinner seven days a week. Operating hours are 5:00 a.m. to 10:00 p.m. on weekdays and 5:00 a.m. to 11:00 p.m. on weekends. There is usually a line out the front door with people waiting to get a seat on weekends at this diner. The only day during the year that the Agawam is closed is Christmas. As stated above, the diner is still being operated by members of the Galanis family, who have periodically updated the interior with new countertops

The Agawam's interior is a step back into the 1950s. But it is not retro; it is all totally real, a perfect showpiece!

and booths. The exterior stainless steel has a few dings, but it retains its 1950s charm. A look at the menu will show the usual breakfast, lunch and dinner options with specials. The prices only recently were raised but are still extremely affordable. Breakfast is served all day, including eggs any style along with omelets, breakfast sandwiches, pancakes and French toast. Lunch and dinner shows chicken potpie, meatloaf and fried chicken, along with fried clams and scallops, veal cutlets, hot turkey sandwiches and various other sandwiches such as hamburgers, clam rolls and tuna or chicken salad. There are also weekly specials served while they last until 8:00 p.m. (check the menu to see the daily specials). The Agawam is justly famous for its selection of freshly baked pies, as it maintains its own in-house bakery in the basement. The chocolate cream, coconut cream and banana cream pies are irresistible. Various other baked goods are available, such as turnovers, brownies and apple squares, along with desserts like bread pudding and Grapenut pudding.

Four Sisters Owl Diner, 244 Appleton Street, Lowell

1940 Worcester Lunch Car

As is the case with a lot of the diners featured in this book, the Four Sisters Owl Diner started out life with a different name at a different location. The Owl Diner, Worcester Lunch Car No. 759, was the flagship for a chain of diners operated by friends and family members of the DeCola brothers of Waltham, Massachusetts. The diner was first delivered to Main Street in Waltham in 1940 and named the Monarch Diner. It originally was built with a partitioned-off kitchen located in the right rear corner of the building. In March 1942, the Worcester Lunch Car Company was asked to remove this kitchen to create more dining area. This happened because a separate addition had been built onto the back of the diner by this time that housed a larger kitchen and, assumedly, restroom facilities. The diner stayed there until being replaced by a larger stainless steel Jerry O'Mahony diner about 1950 or '51. It then was sold and moved to its current location in Lowell. The only real change was to the panels located to the left of the front door that originally had the "Monarch" name. These were changed to say "The Owl." The italicized font that was used for "Monarch" was changed to an old English style for "The Owl." The only reason I can see for the font change

The Four Sisters Owl Diner the way it currently looks, with the larger entryway designed by Richard Gutman. The front of the diner, including the entryway, features all brand-new porcelain-enameled steel panels.

Here is a view of the Owl from 1984 showing the way it looked right up until the new entryway was added.

was space, as the old English style took up less space than the slanted font. It is not clear how many operators the Owl has had since 1950, but I do know that the Zoukis family was operating the diner in the late 1970s and early 1980s before Tom and Marybeth Shanahan bought the place in 1982. Prior to the Owl, they had been leasing the Peerless Diner, also in Lowell, and I believe they had thoughts of buying that diner, but when the Owl came on the market, they jumped at the chance for ownership and have never looked back.

The previous owners did not seem to ever utilize the attached dining room, but this changed when the Shanahans took over, as well they had to. This diner gets packed, especially on weekends. In fact, with this in mind, in the last couple of years, the Shanahans took advantage of a government grant that allowed them to make an upgrade to the diner. This upgrade consisted of the removal of the small, added-on entryway and building a larger vestibule that could accommodate more of an area for customers waiting to be seated in peak business times. To do this, they contacted Richard Gutman, who designed the new structure that would cover a fairly good-sized portion of the front wall, leaving two window/wall sections on the left side and three window/wall sections on the right of the new entryway. Gutman also designed new porcelain steel panels for the front wall and vestibule. Based on the old panels, the graphics were transferred to the new configuration. The words "The Owl" were now placed on the front wall of the vestibule. The right-side "Booth Service" panel was sacrificed so the panels that said "DINER" could fit on that side. The contractor who did the site work did an unbelievable job in re-creating the tile work inside the new vestibule that was on the diner's interior, as well as other details that went into the creation of this new addition.

With their wonderful food and service, the Shanahans have certainly created an institution that is revered by local customers. It has also become a dining destination for patrons who are traveling near (or through) Lowell and tourists here to see the sites of this old mill city. Famous for offering freshly sliced, off-the-bone Virginia ham steak for breakfast, the selections include the usual eggs any style, pancakes, French toast, Belgian waffles and also something that is unique to the Owl: the naming of their omelet selections. Named after streets in the city, there are omelets called Andover Street (the works), Appleton Street (American cheese), Bridge Street (sausage, peppers and cheese) and Chelmsford Street (ham, mushrooms, onions and cheese), along with a dozen more "Street Omelets." As is in most other diners nowadays, breakfast sandwiches are offered, along with specials of corned beef hash with two eggs, toast, home fries and beans; an eight-ounce sirloin steak with one egg, toast and home fries; or two eggs, toast and home fries.

When the Owl was operating as the Monarch Diner in Waltham, it had been delivered from the Worcester Lunch Car Company with a partitioned-off kitchen in the right rear corner of the diner. This was removed when the building acquired a cinder block kitchen addition. Other than that early reconfiguration, the Owl's interior is almost completely original.

Eggs Benedict is another special offered. Other offerings include fresh fruit, muffins, hot and cold cereal and bagels. Breakfast is served all day.

The lunch menu is basically made up of soups, salads, sandwiches, club sandwiches and ten different dinner plates. The dinner plates are served with a choice of mashed potatoes, French fries or home fries, a vegetable, roll and butter. Sandwiches come with French fries, and club sandwiches come with French fries and coleslaw. The soup of the day is served in either a bowl or a cup, and five different salads are available: tossed, Greek, chef's, tuna salad and chicken salad. Dessert selections include pie (plain or with ice cream), strawberry shortcake and various puddings. Dinners and sandwiches are served Monday through Friday, 11:00 a.m. to 2:00 p.m. Hours of operation are Monday through Saturday, 6:00 a.m. to 2:00 p.m., and Sundays, 7:00 a.m. to 2:00 p.m.

NOTE: There are two other diners that are offshoots of the Four Sister's Owl Diner in Massachusetts, both run by members of the same family: the Dream Diner in Tyngsboro (on-site built) and Rosie's Diner in North Chelmsford (storefront diner). Menus and service are similar to that at the Owl.

Chapter 3

South Shore, South Coast and Cape Cod

The Massachusetts region known as the South Shore officially describes the cities and towns that physically border the Atlantic Ocean south of Boston as far as the Cape Cod Canal, basically starting in Quincy and continuing south through towns like Hingham, Weymouth, Hull, Cohasset, Scituate, Marshfield, Duxbury, Kingston and Plymouth. But to the majority of people, unofficially the area continues inland, encompassing towns like Holbrook, Rockland and Pembroke. For the sake of this book, I am extending this section all the way to U.S. Route 1 in the Foxboro/Attleboro area.

Historically, diners in this area were plentiful in the cities of Quincy and Brockton, with a few scattered in between. Places like Braintree, Weymouth and Kingston have had classic diners in years past. State Routes 3 (now Route 3A) and 28 were once the main thoroughfares connecting Boston to Cape Cod and more than likely had their share of diners, but now Route 3A has only the built-on-site Wheelhouse Diner in North Quincy, and you do not even see a diner on Route 28 until you get to Middleboro. Brockton had a couple of diners last into the early 1980s, but one—a 1970 vintage Kullman Colonial-style diner—was already being used as a Bickford's Restaurant, and the Colonial Diner—a late 1930s vintage Sterling Diner on Main Street near downtown—was demolished by 1993.

This chapter will also cover diners on Cape Cod and along the South Coast westward to Attleboro and Plainville. There are two of the oldest diners in Massachusetts here: the Tin Man Diner of North Falmouth, a 1920s Tierney diner (currently closed); and Tex Barry's Coney Island Diner, a mid-1920s Worcester Lunch Car in downtown Attleboro. There are also two of the Bay State's newest diners: Dave's Diner, a 1997 vintage Starlite Diner in Middleboro; and the Juke Box Diner, a 2000 vintage Diner-Mite Diner in Somerset. There are a couple of newly transplanted diners as well. Betsy's Diner in Falmouth and the Patriot Diner in Pocasset are both Mountain View Diners that had previous lives elsewhere. Betsy's came to Massachusetts from Pennsylvania in 1992, and the Patriot came here in 2003 from New Jersey by way of a brief pit stop in Connecticut.

LIST OF DINERS IN REGION

Al Mac's Diner
135 President Avenue, Fall River
DeRaffele Diners

Andy's Rockland Diner
1019 South Main Street, Fall River
Sterling Diners

Bagel Express Café
938 Lees River Avenue, Somerset
Converted train car

Betsy's Diner
457 Main Street, Falmouth
Mountain View Diners

Bickford's Restaurant
37 Oak Street, Brockton
Kullman Diners

Blue Point Restaurant
6 Dayton Street, Acushnet
Worcester Lunch Car Company (No. 748)

The Catman Café
16 Old Colony Way, Mansfield
Sterling Diners

South Shore, South Coast and Cape Cod

Club Car Restaurant
1 Main Street, Nantucket
Converted train car

Dave's Diner
390 West Grove Street, Middleboro
Starlite Diners 1997

Don's Diner
121 South Street, Plainville
Mountain View Diners

50's Diner
900R Providence Highway, Dedham
On-site

Jake's Diner
104 Alden Road, Fairhaven
Jerry O'Mahony Diners

Joe's Diner
51 Broadway, Taunton
Sterling Diners

Jukebox Diner
1155 Grand Army Highway, Somerset
Dinermite Diners

Mill Pond Diner
2571 Cranberry Highway, Wareham
Jerry O'Mahony Diners

Nite Owl Diner
1680 Pleasant Street, Fall River
DeRaffele Diners (closed)

Olympian Diner
17 Hancock Street, Braintree
On-site

Orchid Diner
805 Rockdale Avenue, New Bedford
Jerry O'Mahony Diners

Patriot Diner
808 Mac Arthur Boulevard, Pocasset
Mountain View Diners (closed)

Red Wing Diner
2235 Boston-Providence Highway, Walpole
Worcester Lunch Car Company (No. 709)

Shawmut Diner
943 Shawmut Avenue, New Bedford
Jerry O'Mahony Diners

Sisson's Diner
561 Wareham Street, Route 28, South Middleboro
Converted trolley car (closed)

South Coast Local
81 Fairhaven Road, Mattapoisett
Mountain View Diners

Tex Barry's Coney Island
31 County Street, Attleboro
Worcester Lunch Car Company (No. 542)

Tin Man Diner
70 County Road, North Falmouth
Tierney Diners (closed)

Town Square Diner
164 Nahatan Street, Norwood
On-site

Wheelhouse Diner
453 Hancock Street, North Quincy
On-site

Wheelhouse Diner, 453 Hancock Street, North Quincy

On-site

Historically, the city of Quincy has been home to quite a few diners. Local residents will recall with fondness places like the Mayflower Diner, Pilgrim Diner, Russell's Diner, Peter's Diner and Eddie's Diner. To be sure, there are other restaurants where you can get a decent breakfast and lunch in town, but the Wheelhouse is the only place that calls itself a diner and lives up to the name. The Wheelhouse Diner is actually a regular building that may have started out as something else. Although not factory-built, this place exhibits pretty much the same interior layout, ambiance and menu as anything that was produced by any of the diner manufacturers. It features a counter with stools, a handful of booths and cooking done right behind the counter. Doug Showstead has been manning the grill behind the counter of this diner for the last half dozen years. Showstead offers something one rarely sees nowadays: a grill man who wears his "whites" (the old-style white shirt and pants usually supplied by a commercial linen service). This, for me,

The Wheelhouse Diner, although not a factory-built model, is a diner nonetheless. Sitting at an angle on the corner of Hancock and Haywood Streets, it calls to customers with the recent addition of a vertical diner sign with a neon "EAT" underneath.

On the inside, the Wheelhouse has the typical diner layout, featuring counter and booth service. Also, the cooking is done primarily right behind the counter.

is a real throwback to the past. A native of nearby Dorchester, Doug is very affable and has worked primarily in diners since his teens. His resume reads like a who's who of diners in the area. Starting out at the age of seventeen at the Victoria Diner in Boston, he has worked at various other places like the Mill Pond Diner in Wareham and My Tin Man Diner (when it was in Pocasset). Doug tells me he has fond memories of frequenting the old Englewood Diner, long a neighborhood fixture formerly located near the Ashmont T station in Dorchester's Peabody Square, when he was a kid.

The Wheelhouse is open 5:00 a.m. to 3:00 p.m. seven days a week and offers breakfast and lunch. For breakfast, there are the usual egg dishes, along with three-egg omelets, eggs Benedict and eggs Florentine. There are also pancakes, French toast and waffles, along with the Wheelhouse's version of an English muffin–based sandwich called the Wheelie, which comes five different ways. This is one of the only diners I know that offers a true Irish breakfast. In fact, back in 2008, a quote from the *Boston Globe* stated that "for the best Irish Breakfast this side of the Atlantic, you need only to go as far as the Wheelhouse Diner." If you are not familiar with this dish, an Irish breakfast at the Wheelhouse is composed of two eggs, with white and black blood pudding, banger, Irish bacon, fried tomatoes, home fries and toast. For a dollar more, you can get an order of Irish soda bread with this breakfast. To be fair, they also have an Italian breakfast, which is three eggs scrambled with Italian sausage, pepperoni, peppers, onions and mushrooms, topped with provolone cheese and served with home fries and toast. Breakfast sides include the typical bacon, ham and corned beef hash, along with Irish bacon, sausage, blood pudding and soda bread. The lunch menu has hot and cold sandwiches served with potato chips and a pickle. They recently started offering any of their lunch sandwiches in a sub roll. There is also a variety of club sandwiches and Wheelhouse burgers, which are all served with French fries and a pickle. Daily specials are featured along with soups, salads and desserts. These are usually posted on the "Specials" boards and can change from day to day. Dinner specials include roast turkey, fish and chips, baked meatloaf and chicken parmesan with penne pasta, with many more that can be available on any given day. A good selection of fresh vegetables is offered to go along with the dinners. Soup specials like chicken rice, chicken vegetable and clam chowder (in a cup or a bowl) are offered. Desserts include tapioca and rice pudding, as well as apple, blueberry and lemon meringue pies. There is also a "Sinfully Chocolate Cake" offered.

Betsy's Diner, 457 Main Street, Falmouth

1950s Mountain View Diner

Betsy's Diner spent most of its earlier life as the Peter Pan Diner in Kuhnsville, Pennsylvania. By the late 1980s, the diner had acquired a red mansard roof and was operating as Chris's Family Restaurant before the owners upgraded to a used environmental-style Swingle diner that had previously operated in Hamburg, Pennsylvania. This was the former Pot of Gold Diner, which had a highly visible location adjacent to an exit of I-78. The Pot of Gold Diner went out of business at the Hamburg location and was bought by the people running the former Peter Pan. It was placed next door to the older diner, and the 1950s Mountain View Diner (No. 498) remained on site and closed until Larry Holmes of Winthrop, Massachusetts, came into the picture.

At the time, Holmes was operating two other restaurants in the town of Winthrop (near Boston) and had been trying to get into the diner business for quite some time. He actually had bought an older Worcester Lunch Car that last operated in Buzzard's Bay, Massachusetts, in the late 1980s and had that moved into storage while attempting to locate a decent operating location.

Betsy's Diner is a nicely maintained Mountain View Diner. The attached building on the left was half of an existing building that was at this location prior to the diner. The right side of the building was cut away and moved to the back of the property. The remaining structure was converted to a dining room for the restaurant.

The plans for that diner never came to fruition, and he resold it after a short period of time. In 1992, I heard from Richard Gutman that Holmes had purchased the former Peter Pan Diner. It was delivered in June of that same year to the Main Street location in Falmouth at the site of an existing restaurant that had closed. The diner, made up of two sections along with an entryway, sat in the parking lot while contractors readied the site.

The first thing Holmes had them do was alter the existing building by chopping off the right half of the structure and moving it to the back of the property as a storage facility. The front of the diner was moved and attached to the right side of the existing building. The rear section of the diner was placed behind the diner, and the entryway was reattached with a new configuration. Instead of the door to the vestibule being on the front elevation with windows on the two side walls, Holmes had the doors placed on the sides and a window on the front. He also used some stainless steel and enamel stripes from the left side of the diner to cover the front of the existing building that now would be used for a dining room. This gave the complex a cohesive look, at least from the front. The diner opened that fall as Betsy's, named after Holmes's mother. The Holmes family operated the diner for

The interior of Betsy's Diner is pretty much the way it has always been since it came out of the Mountain View factory. Falmouth is a major vacation town on Cape Cod, and the diner gets pretty busy during the summer months.

a couple of years and then sold it to Dave and Karen Chandler, who have been operating it successfully since 1994.

Betsy's slogan is "Good Food, Not Fast Food—Eat Heavy," and the word "heavy" is repeated often throughout the menu. Breakfast is served all day, and the breakfast dishes—which they refer to as their "Heavy Hitters"— are numbered 1 through 9. For example, #1 is one egg with toast and home fries, and #1½ is two eggs with toast and home fries. #9 is Betsy's Super Platter, which features two eggs, two pancakes, toast and home fries, bacon, sausage or ham. They also have pancakes, filled pancakes, French toast and three-egg omelets. Waffles are only offered 6:00 a.m. to 11:00 a.m. Many breakfast side orders are available, including assorted home-baked muffins, baked beans and the not-so-common brown bread with raisins. The lunch and dinner menu is available from 11:30 a.m. daily and features a huge selection. Burgers, made from half a pound of ground sirloin, are char-grilled and come with lettuce, tomato and onion on a roll. The customer who wants a cheeseburger has a choice of American, Swiss or cheddar cheese. Additions of grilled onions, mushrooms or peppers are fifty cents each, and bacon, ham, blue cheese or chili are one dollar each. A large selection of sandwiches is served on white, wheat, rye and scali breads or a roll. Club sandwiches of roast turkey, roast beef, ham, tuna and hamburger are served with French fries. A half sandwich and soup is available also. Fish selections include everything from a fried clam strip roll or plate, fried fish sandwich or fish and chips to fried crab cakes and beans, broiled scrod and a char-grilled eight-ounce swordfish steak. Seasonal favorites on the daily specials include fried clams, scallops and a lobster roll. Dinners, referred to as "Heavy D's," include liver and onions with bacon, chicken, ziti and broccoli, char-grilled combo steak tips and linguica, among many others. All soups are homemade (by the cup or bowl). Salads are listed, as well as a children's menu, "Little Diners." There are also assorted pies, cakes, muffins and puddings available daily.

Be aware that the operating hours for Betsy's Diner may change with the season, as it is in a resort area on Cape Cod. The hours for springtime are Monday through Saturday, 6:00 a.m. to 7:00 p.m., and Sundays are 7:00 a.m. to 2:00 p.m. Summer hours are Monday through Thursday (and Saturday), 6:00 a.m. to 7:30 p.m., and 6:00 a.m. to 8:00 p.m. on Friday. Sundays stay the same as springtime hours.

SHAWMUT DINER, 943 SHAWMUT AVENUE, NEW BEDFORD

1954 Jerry O'Mahony Diner

My first introduction to the Shawmut Diner was through a Massachusetts State Lottery commercial that aired on TV, circa 1981. The commercial showed a truck driver stopping at this great-looking 1950s stainless steel diner with a nice neon sign on the roof to play the lottery. I had never seen or heard of this diner before and wondered where it was. Not long after seeing this, I was talking to my newly acquainted "diner pal" David Hebb about it, and he told me he knew the diner. So, on June 19, 1982, I made a trip down to New Bedford (with Dave and his girlfriend, Sally) to see the Shawmut Diner myself. We got out of my van and started taking pictures of the diner. Just then, a nice lady came out of the front door of the diner and informed us, "Anyone taking pictures of this diner has to come in for a free cup of coffee!" We laughed and went inside, where we met Celeste Paleologos, co-owner with her husband, Phil. They had purchased the diner a little over a year before, in February 1981, to be precise. Phil has since told me that when they bought the diner, it was a

Thanks to owners Phil and Celeste Paleologos, the Shawmut Diner has become a destination not only for the regular local clientele but for travelers as well. The exterior is in quite decent shape for a late-model Jerry O'Mahony diner.

little worse for the wear, to say the least. It turned out to be a diamond in the rough, and after a thorough cleaning and sprucing up (which, incidentally, got rid of the lottery machine by the cashier stand), they reopened, bringing the diner back to life with a vengeance. Due to Phil and Celeste's hard work, not to mention the extreme friendliness they exude, this is one of the best diners in Massachusetts, no holds barred. The Paleologoses and their staff make you feel at home, whether you are a first-time customer or a longtime regular.

Phil tells me the original owners of this 1954 vintage Jerry O'Mahony–built diner were Jack and Mary Mello. The Mellos had already been operating the Green Diner, a barrel-roofed Worcester Lunch Car located on Rockdale Avenue near the Clarks Cove area of New Bedford, in the year prior to buying the Shawmut. They operated both diners simultaneously until 1960, when they decided to concentrate on one location. The Green Diner ended up being run by other family members, and Mary Mello continued with the Shawmut for a few years after Jack passed away. Toward the end of the 1960s, Mary stepped away from running the diner and leased it out to at least three different operators over the next ten years. Unfortunately,

Phil Paleologos is not only a diner owner, he is also a radio broadcast professional. At one time, Phil had a syndicated radio talk show that originated from inside the Shawmut Diner called *The Diner Show*. Phil had a small broadcast booth built into the left rear corner of the diner (just out of view on the left). He would engage in conversations with phone-in guests and also step out of the booth from time to time during his show to get the customers' opinions on the issues of the day.

these managers let the diner's appearance, as well as reputation, slide. This is where Phil and Celeste came in, and the rest, as they say, is history.

Located conveniently off state highway Route 140 at the Hathaway Road exit, the diner is at the corner of Hathaway Road and Shawmut Avenue. Open long hours, the menu is quite extensive, serving breakfast, lunch and dinner. Breakfast is served anytime, and there are many items to choose from. There are the typical egg dishes (one egg or two eggs) with choice of sides like bacon, ham, sausage, linguica, Canadian bacon, corned beef hash or sirloin steak. There is a "create your own omelet" section, with fillings that encompass the above-mentioned sides as well as chili, peppers, onions, mushrooms, spinach, broccoli or salsa, along with cheddar, Swiss, American or feta cheeses. There are also classic omelets available, like the western, Cajun, Mexican, Greek, southwestern and Portuguese. Waffles, pancakes and French toast are represented, along with breakfast specials that are reasonably priced and feature items as varied as sausage gravy and biscuit, country fried steak and eggs and a grilled potato melt. There is even homemade fried dough topped with your choice of plain sugar, powdered sugar or cinnamon sugar. Various other sides include cereal (hot and cold), fresh melon wedges, half a grapefruit, bagels (with cream cheese if so desired) and grits, along with banana nut bread, sweet roll and something that is extremely popular: a cheese roll. I asked Phil about this particular item and he explained. The Shawmut Diner's famous cheese roll has a history and tradition that goes back to when the diner first opened its doors in 1954. Original owners Jack and Mary Mello were first-rate bakers. They created from scratch a mini loaf of freshly baked bread, shaped somewhat like a small football. Inside this mouthwatering creation, they folded into the dough chunks of aged cheddar and Romano cheese, baking it to a golden brown perfection. But the real magic occurred when the cheese roll was sliced and grilled until the cheeses formed a melt-in-your-mouth crust. That same recipe is still used today, satisfying new generations of cheese roll lovers. Breakfast sandwiches and wraps round out this part of the menu. The sandwiches are served on toast or English muffins, although bagels can be substituted for fifty cents more. If one is feeling adventurous, a cheese roll can be substituted for two dollars more.

The lunch/dinner menu has appetizers and sides, including buffalo chicken tenders, chicken (or) cheese quesadillas and a couple of items you do not see too often—French meat pie (by the slice) and a spicy stuffed quahog. French fries and onion rings are offered also. Salads include a garden salad (large), side salad (small), Greek salad, chef salad, grilled chicken salad, buffalo chicken salad and tuna salad. Sandwiches run the gamut from an eight-ounce Angus beef burger or cheeseburger and even an Angus bacon burger to a Philly steak and cheese, sliced Virginia ham and cheese, grilled linguica and homemade meatloaf sandwich, among others. These are served on a bulkie roll or choice of bread. Several club sandwiches and wraps are available, along with two open-faced sandwiches: hot turkey or pot roast.

Being that this diner is located in the old fishing port of New Bedford, seafood dishes are served, including New Bedford fish and chips (small or large portions are available), broiled scrod (regular or Portuguese style) and a tuna salad plate. Poultry dishes include "Fresh off the Bone" roasted turkey, southern fried boneless chicken, grilled chicken and a buffalo chicken dinner. Beef dishes include sirloin steak, homemade pot roast, country fried steak, chopped hamburger steak and onions and grilled baby beef liver. "Shawmut Favorites" include a shepherd's pie casserole, French meat pie, baked Virginia ham, franks and beans or linguica and beans, as well as meatloaf.

All the above dinners come with a cup of soup, potato and vegetable, as well as bread and butter. Add one dollar for chowder or a side salad. Desserts include a Sno-Ball, which is deep-fried ice cream with strawberries and whipped cream, and a brownie sundae, as well as "Desserts of the Day."

The Shawmut is open Monday through Thursday, 5:30 a.m. to 2:30 p.m., and day and night from Friday at 5:30 a.m. to Sunday at 3:00 p.m. Christmas was traditionally the only day the diner closed until this past year, when Phil and Celeste decided to open for breakfast and were pleasantly surprised to see the diner packed with customers. So Phil tells me that it looks like they will start a new tradition of opening on Christmas morning for the people out and about looking for breakfast.

AL MAC'S DINER-RESTAURANT, 135 PRESIDENT AVENUE, FALL RIVER

1953 DeRaffele Diner

The slogan on Al Mac's sign says "Justly Famous Since 1910." This underlines the fact that the name "Al McDermott" has been associated with diners in the Fall River area for just over a century. Mr. McDermott first entered the food service industry as the proprietor of a horse-drawn lunch wagon in 1910. According to Richard Gutman's book, *American Diner Then & Now*, it has been said that Al Mac (as he was universally known) bought so many diners over the years that family members lost count of the actual tally. There are certainly more than a few diners still in existence that were once owned by him. Two examples are Gilley's Lunch Cart in Portsmouth, New Hampshire, and the former Tommy's Deluxe Diner, which operated in Middletown, Rhode Island, for many years. Tommy's is currently living another life as the Road Island Diner in Oakley, Utah, after undergoing a complete stripped-to-the-frame restoration by entrepreneur Keith Walker. The current Al Mac's Diner, a 1953 vintage DeRaffele diner, was the last one purchased by the lifelong diner man, who passed away in the 1970s. Since 1989, the diner has been co-owned by Norm Gauthier, his daughter Dawn Xanyn and son-in-law Garet Xanyn. According to Dawn Xanyn, Al Mac's Diner is noted for "home-style cooking." They serve "real" turkey (not processed), and their meatloaf and meatballs, along with most of their menu, are homemade. They strive to present their product in a manner that reminds patrons of home.

Al Mac's Diner Restaurant in Fall River was picked up and turned ninety degrees circa 1989, when a new strip mall was built on property adjacent to the diner. This is the way it looks today, with its restored signage that proclaims "Justly Famous Since 1910."

Other than newer booths and tables, the interior of Al Mac's has not changed much since it was delivered from New Rochelle, New York, in 1953.

Breakfast is served all day, and the breakfast menu features eggs any style, complemented with your choice of bacon, ham, sausage (three links or two patties), Italian sausage, corned beef hash, chourico and sirloin steak. They have a large selection of omelets, including the usual eastern (ham and peppers), western (ham, onions and peppers) and a twist on the western—a Portuguese western (chourico, onions and peppers)—as well as Florentine, Spanish and Greek, among others. There is also an Al Mac's Special Omelet that includes any six ingredients. Other items include breakfast sandwiches, pancakes (buttermilk, blueberry or chocolate chip), Texas French toast and raisin bread French toast, along with Belgian waffles. But that's not all; there is also a "Specials Menu" served Monday through Friday, 7:00 a.m. to 11:00 a.m. (not available on holidays).

Lunch features a large selection of sandwiches, club sandwiches, burgers, steaks and roll-ups. There are two kinds of hot dogs: a "Slim Jim" and a "Foot Long." Salads include garden, chef, Caesar and Greek, and the soup du jour is available by the cup or bowl. In addition to the regular sandwiches on the lunch menu, sandwich specials are also served Monday through Friday, 11:00 a.m. to 3:00 p.m. These specials come with fries or onion rings (add twenty-five cents for onion rings instead of fries), dill slices and a soft drink, and soft drink refills are available for one dollar each. The sandwich specials include soup and sandwich (choice of egg salad or grilled cheese prepared on white or wheat bread) or two Slim Jim hot dogs, clam strip roll, chicken salad roll, tuna salad roll or BLT. There are also five kinds of eight-inch submarine sandwiches on the specials menu.

There are six different dinners offered for $7.99, including items like spaghetti and Italian sausage with garlic roll and meatloaf dinner with potato and vegetable, among others. There are seven dinners for $8.99, including chopped sirloin with potato and vegetable and liver with potato and vegetable. There are three dinners for $9.99: home-style turkey dinner with bread stuffing, potato, vegetable and cranberry sauce; fried chicken dinner with potato, vegetable and cranberry sauce; and country fried cube steak dinner with potato and vegetable. For most of these dinners, there are smaller portions available at a dollar off the regular price. There is a choice of potato that includes real (not instant) mashed, fried or baked, as well as rice of the day. Additionally, Dawn Xanyn says they sell some local favorites like Portuguese steak, New England pot roast, corned beef and cabbage, boneless fried chicken, chicken or turkey potpie and shepherd's pie on certain days. They try to place additional specials on a daily basis (Sundays and holidays excluded), and summer brings a rotation of cold salad options like potato salad, macaroni salad, Greek pasta salad and Italian pasta salad, which are offered in lieu of potato or vegetable. There is also a children's menu available, as well as kid-sized desserts for those ten years and under.

Appetizers/sides include French fries, onion rings, mozzarella sticks and potato skins, as well as jalapeño poppers, chicken tenders and buffalo tenders. There is also a combo plate (two potato skins, three poppers, three tenders, three mozzarella sticks) with sour cream, marinara, BBQ sauce and sweet and sour. Dinner sides include cranberry or apple sauce, garlic bread and coleslaw, among others. Desserts featured include chocolate, vanilla and Grapenut pudding, along with various pies and cakes.

Al Mac's Diner is open Monday through Wednesday, 6:30 a.m. to 3:00 p.m., and Thursday from 6:30 a.m. to 9:00 p.m. On Fridays, the diner opens at 6:30 a.m. and does not close until Sunday at 3:00 p.m.

Don's Diner, South Street, Plainville

1950s Mountain View Diner

The current Don's Diner is the third diner at this location in downtown Plainville. The first diner was a small 1920s vintage Worcester Lunch Car originally operated as Alicia's Diner before Donald R. Perreault took over the reins on January 21, 1936. He immediately changed the name to Don's Diner and threw away the keys, running the establishment as a twenty-four-hour business. In 1940, Don saw there was a growing demand for good food and convinced the owners of many of the area businesses to allow him to deliver food to their employees for coffee breaks, making the deliveries in his own car and carrying the food into the factories in large baskets. The Perreault family believes they may have been the first on the East Coast to begin such a catering service. The catering business was successful enough by the late 1940s that it had caught the attention of Bill Rosenberg. Rosenberg, along with other family members (including his brother-in-law, Harry Winokur), had started Industrial Luncheon Service in Quincy, another company catering to local businesses. (This company later branched out into a little business called Dunkin' Donuts.) Rosenberg had approached the Perreaults about the possibility of buying the catering business from them. The Perreaults declined Rosenberg's offer.

Don's son, Donald W. Perreault, joined the business in October 1958. About 1961, a fire claimed the original diner, and the Perreaults bought the former Mancini's Service Diner (Worcester Lunch Car No. 791) that was

Don's Diner in Plainville got an environmental remodeling in the early 1990s. Back then, the Perreault family decided that the original stainless steel façade had seen better days and the cost of trying to duplicate it would probably be too expensive. So they went with some vinyl siding and a mansard roof, keeping some stainless steel trim around the windows and corners.

Here we see Don's Diner from the early 1980s with the original façade intact. This is the third diner to be called Don's at this same location. Formerly known as the Minuteman Diner, it was located on U.S. Route 1 in nearby Attleboro and was moved here in 1969.

located in Providence, Rhode Island, to operate as the second Don's Diner. It was operated as Don's until 1969, when the family upgraded again, this time to the current (third) diner, a 1950s Mountain View Diner that had previously traded as the Minuteman Diner on U.S. Route 1 in nearby Attleboro.

The Perreaults kept this diner in original condition until the early 1990s, when they decided to freshen up the façade. They removed the stainless steel and red striped panels under the windows and replaced them with vinyl siding. They also covered the top with an environmental mansard roof, but there is still enough stainless steel trim around the windows and at the corners to identify its pedigree as a 1950s modern stainless diner. The interior remains fairly original, with the exception of newer booths. The diner is currently in the hands of the third generation, Don W.'s son, Perry M. Perreault.

No longer open twenty-four hours, the diner operates 6:00 a.m. to 2:00 p.m. Tuesday through Friday and 7:00 a.m. to 1:00 p.m. on Saturday and Sunday (Sunday is breakfast only). Don's is closed on Mondays. The menu is made up of the usual suspects: eggs cooked any style, breakfast sandwiches on English muffin or bagel and French toast, as well as pancakes (plain or

Inside Don's Diner, the styling of this Mountain View Diner is quite intact. The booths are newer, and all cooking is done in the attached kitchen. The Perreaults have quite a few old photos of the diner and other places in town displayed in picture frames, as well as within the glass-fronted menu boards on the hood over the back bar.

with blueberries). Breakfast sides include bacon, ham, sausage, kielbasa or chourico, and home fried potatoes are generally included with your choice of toast. Lunch choices are mostly sandwiches on various breads and wraps, usually with chips and pickles, but substitutions of French fries or onion rings for chips is an additional dollar. They also have hot submarine sandwiches, as well as sandwiches on bulkie rolls that come with fries and pickles.

TEX BARRY'S CONEY ISLAND, 31 COUNTY STREET, ATTLEBORO

1920s Worcester Lunch Car

The diner now known as Tex Barry's Coney Island on County Street in Attleboro has had many names over the years since it was built in the late 1920s. Prior to the time I found it in September 1981, it had traded as the Central Diner (1931–36), County Diner (1936–37), Modern Diner (1939–40), Victory Diner (1946), Burne Diner (1953), G&J Diner (1958–74), Brillon's Diner (1975), Ralph's Diner (1977), Granny's Kitchen (1980) and

Tex Barry's Coney Island Hot Dogs is housed in a mid- to late 1920s vintage Worcester Lunch Car that is set end-wise to the street, hard up against the banks of the Ten Mile River.

Desi's Diner (1981). The actual business called Tex Barry's has a unique history that was outlined to me by the current owner of the Attleboro shop, Arthur Bombadier.

Tex Barry's Coney Island was a franchised business started back in the mid- to late 1960s by three brothers: Joe, Altino and Tony Costa. The first shop opened in Somerset, and from that point, they opened a total of fourteen shops in southeastern Massachusetts and Rhode Island. The "Tex Barry's" name came from brother Altino. It was a name he went under while racing at Seekonk Speedway. Eventually, the business relationship fell apart due to bickering between the brothers, and they decided to divide the shops among themselves. Brockton, Taunton, Attleboro, Somerset, Fall River and Swansea, Massachusetts, as well as Newport, Rhode Island, are locations that Arthur Bombadier can recall with certainty. Today, there are only two left: Attleboro and Taunton. The Taunton shop is owned by Tony Medeiros. From what we know, the Attleboro shop was the only one ever located in a diner. Tex Barry's Coney Island is known for its sauce, which, from what Arthur tells me, came from a recipe made by the Costa brothers' mom.

In 1977, Arthur's mother, Connie, started working for Tex Barry's at its old location on 6 Union Street, behind the post office. According to Arthur, at that time Tony Costa was in charge of the Attleboro, Taunton and Brockton shops. Things were already bad when Connie started working for Joe Aguiar, who held the franchise for the Attleboro shop. This shop was housed in an early 1920s vintage Worcester Lunch Car that had seen better days. By 1979, Joe was running the shop into the ground. The gas had already been shut off, and Joe was actually using sternos to cook with. Arthur says, "I can remember seeing two to three sternos under the hot dog grill and four sternos under the steam box. Also, the hamburger grill was out of commission." Not long after this, the electric company came and shut the power off, and the shop was closed.

Within a couple of weeks of Tex Barry's closing, Connie received a call from Tony Costa asking her if she would be interested in owning a Tex Barry's franchise. She talked with the family about it, and after borrowing money from her sister Rita, she decided to go for it. In September 1979, she reopened the shop, with Arthur and her sister helping out. After a year of operating the shop, the city decided it wanted to revitalize the Union Street area with a new city hall and police station. In 1982, there were a few stores that were removed by eminent domain; Tex Barry's was one of them. The shop moved, coincidentally, into another old Worcester Lunch Car (No. 542) located just around the corner at 31 County Street, where it is today. Arthur

Tex Barry's interior features the original ceramic tile floor and counter apron, as well as the Monel Metal Hood over the cooking area. Monel was a nickel-plated copper that predated the use of stainless steel. Tex Barry's menu is pretty simple—just hot dogs, hamburgers and French fries—all at an extremely reasonable price.

has been running the business since 1985, when Connie became ill and was not able to return to work. That same year, Tony Costa decided it was time to retire and move to Florida and wanted to sell all three of his shops. He gave Arthur the first option to buy the Attleboro shop from him. This seems to have been the right decision, as the business has been going strong for the past twenty-six years under Arthur's ownership.

Tex Barry's Coney Island is not open for breakfast. The menu consists simply of hot dogs, hamburgers and French fries, along with assorted beverages of soda and bottled water. Hours of operation are 10:00 a.m. to 8:00 p.m. Monday through Friday, 10:00 a.m. to 3:00 p.m. on Saturdays and closed on Sundays.

Chapter 4

MetroWest and Central Massachusetts

Historically, apart from Boston and some of the eastern manufacturing cities and towns, the MetroWest suburbs and central Massachusetts area have held their own with a large number of diners still in existence. This is mostly due to the fact that Worcester, the second largest city in the Bay State, was the birthplace of the diner-building industry and also home to a large manufacturing center for various industries. In fact, looking at the list below, currently there seems to be a higher concentration of diners here than any other region in the state, especially of Worcester Lunch Car Company–built diners. One of the oldest in the country, Casey's Diner in Natick, dates to 1921. It has been run by four generations of the Casey family since they bought it used in the mid-1920s. There are two rare-for-Massachusetts Silk City diners located here: Tim's Diner in Leominster and Lou-Roc's Diner in Worcester. Both have been altered, especially on the outside—Tim's due to a couple of automobile accidents and Lou-Roc's because a former owner thought it would look better completely hidden from view. In that particular instance, there is no accounting for taste! There is also a fairly new development here, in Worcester of all places. An outlet of a national diner chain that started in the southwestern USA, a 5 & Diner was opened within the last five years. These 5 & Diners are built on-site but look like stylized versions of retro 1950s diners.

LIST OF DINERS IN REGION

Airport Diner
108 Lancaster Road, Shirley
Worcester Lunch Car Company

Blanchard's 101 Diner
322 Cambridge Street, Worcester
Worcester Lunch Car Company

Blue Moon Diner
102 Main Street, Gardner
Worcester Lunch Car Company (No. 815)

Boulevard Diner
155 Shrewsbury Street, Worcester
Worcester Lunch Car Company (No. 730)

Carl's Oxford Diner
291 Main Street, Oxford
Worcester Lunch Car Company

Carmen's Diner
135 Lunenburg Street, Fitchburg
Worcester Lunch Car Company

Casey's Diner
36 South Avenue, Natick
Worcester Lunch Car Company

Central Diner
90 Elm Street, Millbury
Worcester Lunch Car Company (No. 673)

Charlie's Diner
5 Meadow Road, Spencer
Worcester Lunch Car Company (No. 816)

Chet's Diner
191 Main Street, Northboro
On-site

Claudette's 1921 Diner
59 Shrewsbury Street, Boylston
Worcester Lunch Car Company (No. 586)

Corner Lunch
133 Lamartine Street, Worcester
DeRaffele/Musi

Dinky's Blue Belle Diner
70 Clinton Street, Shrewsbury
Worcester Lunch Car Company (No. 814)

The Edge
51 Hartford Pike, Shrewsbury
Fodero Diners

Emerald Isle Diner
49 Millbury Street, Worcester
Jerry O'Mahony Diners

50-50 Diner
440 River Street, Fitchburg
Worcester Lunch Car Company

5 & Diner
525 Lincoln Street, Worcester
On-site

George's Green Island Diner
162 Millbury Street, Worcester
Worcester Lunch Car Company

Gracie's Diner
595 South Main Street, Webster
Worcester Lunch Car Company (No. 682)

Jim's Flying Diner
220 Airport Access Road, Southbridge
Master Diners

Kenmore Diner
250 Franklin Street, Worcester
On-site

Kenwood Diner
97 Main Street, Spencer
Worcester Lunch Car Company (No. 713)

Lloyd's Diner
184 Fountain Street, Framingham
Worcester Lunch Car Company (No. 749)

Lou-Roc's Diner
1074 West Boylston Street, Worcester
Silk City Diners

Lou's Diner
100 Chestnut Street, Clinton
Worcester Lunch Car Company (No. 638)

Main Street Diner
311 Main Street, Athol
Worcester Lunch Car Company

Miss Mendon Diner
16 Uxbridge Road, Mendon
Worcester Lunch Car Company (No. 823)

Miss Worcester Diner
300 Southbridge Street
Worcester Lunch Car Company (No. 812)

Moran Square Diner
6 Myrtle Avenue, Fitchburg
Worcester Lunch Car Company (No. 765)

Parkway Diner
148 Shrewsbury Street, Worcester
Worcester Lunch Car Company (No. 670)

Peg's Diner
87 Church Street, Whitinsville
Worcester Lunch Car Company (No. 723)

Plouffe's Yankee Diner
16 Worcester Road, Charlton
Worcester Lunch Car Company (No. 735)

Ralph's Chadwick Square Diner
95 Prescott Street, Worcester
Worcester Lunch Car Company (No. 660)

Stewart's Diner & Catering
148 Main Street, Blackstone
Worcester Lunch Car Company

Tim's Diner
14 Water Street, Leominster
Silk City Diners (No. 4921)

Tropical Café at White City Diner
22 Rawlins Avenue, Marlboro
Worcester Lunch Car Company (No. 801)

TIM'S DINER, WATER STREET, LEOMINSTER

1949 Silk City Diner

Tim's Diner is one of the smallest (if not the smallest) Silk City diner ever built. This diner's serial number (No. 4921) tells us that it was the twenty-first diner built in 1949 by the Paterson Vehicle Company (makers of the Silk City diner). Originally owned by Roy Hemingway and operated as Roy's Diner, it was bought by Tim Kamataris Sr. in 1953 and has been known as Tim's Diner ever since. There are thirteen stools at the main counter and six more

Tim's Diner is a Silk City Diner, which is extremely rare in the Commonwealth of Massachusetts. Also rare is the size of this diner. It is quite possibly the smallest diner ever built by the Paterson Vehicle Company. The brickwork on the façade was added after a couple of automobile accidents damaged the diner.

In this view, we can see the diner prior to the accidents, circa 1981. This diner's original name was Roy's Diner when it was delivered in 1949.

at the small shelf to the left of the front door as you come in. There are two four-person booths on the right side of the front door and additional seating for up to twenty-two people in the dining room behind the diner itself.

In the early 1980s, the diner's façade was all original, but a couple of auto accidents changed the look of the diner. The entryway was sheared off in the first accident, and there was also extensive damage to the stainless steel skin under the front windows. The entryway was at that point replaced with a small brick-covered one, and brick was added to the façade under the windows. A second accident a short time later smashed in the new brick wall slightly to the right of the entryway. That damage is sort of hidden by the newspaper vending machines standing in front, but there is more evidence on the inside, as the tile wall is bowed in here.

The interior stayed pretty much in original condition other than a recent modification to the cooking hood and ventilation system required by the city building codes. The diner's biggest claim to fame food-wise is its fish chowder. Tim Sr. developed a fish base for his famous chowder that the locals seemingly cannot get enough of. The diner is currently operated by Tim Jr., and he carries on his dad's tradition of offering great breakfasts and

Inside Tim's Diner, everything is pretty much the way it has always been, with the exception of a new ventilating hood over the grill that was mandated by city health, fire and safety codes. The contractor who did the work removed a section of the original hood and fit the new one into the vacant spot as sympathetically as possible.

lunches that do not break your budget. If you go, be aware that the diner's hours are a little different than others: Monday through Friday 4:30 a.m. to 1:00 p.m., Saturday 4:30 a.m. to 10:00 a.m. and Sunday 5:30 a.m. to 11:00 a.m. (no lunch is served on Saturday and Sunday). Breakfasts are big here, with all the usual egg dishes offered, as well as pancakes and French toast. One example of a breakfast special is a steak and cheese omelet. For lunch, one might find a steak and cheese grinder, a chicken finger sandwich with French fries or a chicken finger plate with French fries and Grapenut pudding for desert. And don't forget the fish chowder!

BOULEVARD DINER, SHREWSBURY STREET, WORCESTER

1936 Worcester Lunch Car

The Boulevard Diner is without a doubt *the* showplace diner in a diner city. Looking almost like it just came out of the factory, it is virtually a museum piece, with only some wear and tear to show its age. This diner is lovingly maintained by the George family. The exterior has the trademark porcelain-

The classic looks of the Boulevard Diner in Worcester, with its porcelain enamel, leaded glass and neon signage, make it a winner. Not only that, the food is some of the best you can get anywhere.

enameled steel panels with the name baked right in, and it is also loaded with neon—a three-color stripe that runs along the roofline just above the windows with a neon-ringed clock in the middle, complemented by an equally old neon sign hanging off a pole by the right-hand end of the diner. It is especially fantastic to see when you are coming down the street at night, like an oasis in the dark. The Boulevard Diner was originally bought by Fred J. Galanto in 1936, replacing a smaller 1920s vintage diner. He operated this newer version for the next twenty-nine years before he sold the business circa 1965 to John "Ringo" George, a longtime employee who recalled seeing the diner being delivered to its Shrewsbury Street address when he was a kid.

George operated the diner with a partner until 1969, when the partner left to pursue other endeavors. After John George's death in the early 1990s, his family continued the operation of the diner. In 1999, son Jim George assumed ownership from his mother. Jim and various family members, including his niece, Lisa Carenzo, have been doing a fantastic job in keeping up the quality of both the food and the service. Lisa has been taking on more of the kitchen prep and cooking duties recently, using all the same family recipes. Jim also tells me he has begun making his own Italian sausages again after years of buying them from a local business. The diner is open

Not only does this 1936 vintage Worcester lunch car look good from the outside, but the inside is also museum quality. The George family keeps this place in tiptop condition. Don't miss the Italian specialties at this diner.

twenty-four hours a day (except on Sundays, when it's closed from 3:00 p.m. to 5:00 p.m.). The full menu is available all day, and it is known for its Italian specialties (as well as great American dishes). I have always found that whatever time of the day, it is a good bet that any meal ordered will be a satisfactory one.

All breakfasts with eggs are served with home fries and toast, and side order selections consist of the usual ham, bacon or sausage, but Italian sausage and kielbasa are also available. Like a lot of diners in the city of Worcester, it offers an Italian breakfast (my favorite), which is three eggs with either a homemade Italian sausage or meatball. It also offers a "create your own three-egg omelet" with various ingredients. There are even omelets named after the area colleges, such as the Becker, Holy Cross, Worcester State, the Clark, WPI (Worcester Polytechnic Institute), Quinsig (Quinsigamond Community College) and the Assumption Grey Hound. Pancakes and French toast round out the breakfast menu.

The lunch/dinner menu features a great selection of hot and cold sandwiches (too many to list). Chicken soup and pasta fagioli are always available by the cup or bowl. All the Italian specialty plates are served with ziti or spaghetti. These include meatballs, sausage, eggplant parm, chicken parm and veal parm. There are also cheese and meat ravioli dishes, along with lasagna, eggplant rolletini, manicotti and stuffed shells. Regular American dinners include ribeye steak, Salisbury steak, liver and onions and meatloaf (these all come with mashed potatoes and vegetables, along with bread & butter). Fishcakes and beans and franks and beans are also listed, along with a half dozen appetizers. Catering services are available with twenty-four-hour notice.

CHARLIE'S DINER, 5 MEADOW ROAD, SPENCER

1948 Worcester Lunch Car

Charlie's Diner was started circa 1950 on Plantation Street in Worcester, when Charlie Turner Sr. bought a reconditioned diner (No. 586) from the Worcester Lunch Car Co. The diner had originally been Fahey's Diner of Allston, Massachusetts (1928–37) and then the Adams Diner in Adams, Massachusetts (1937–49). After leaving Adams, it went back to the Worcester factory, where it was updated to become Charlie's Diner. Charlie Turner upgraded to the current diner in 1960. This was Worcester Lunch

Car No. 816, which started out life as Aiken's Mill Pond Diner in Wareham, Massachusetts. Sometime in the 1950s, the Aiken family sold the business to Ernest Blanchard, who replaced the 1948 vintage Worcester car in 1960 with a slightly used stainless steel Jerry O'Mahony diner that had operated in Fall River as Earnshaw's Diner and sold No. 816 to the Turner family. The Turners (now Charlie Jr. and son Steve) operated this diner at the Worcester location until they were forced out by their landlord in 2002. They had hoped to keep the diner in Worcester, but things did not go their way, and the diner stayed in storage for about three years. Finally, in 2005, a new operating location was secured in the nearby town of Spencer. Within a year, the diner was set up on a new foundation with an attached kitchen and restrooms and reopened for business. In 2010, another addition was made to the structure that features a large bar and grill pub.

The menu selections at Charlie's are the normal breakfast and lunch, including soups and salads. Breakfast is served daily until 3:00 p.m. and features the usual eggs, omelets, French toast and pancake dishes. Being that this diner operated most of its life in Worcester, it offers the infamous Italian breakfast that many other diners in the area have (Boulevard, Parkway and

Charlie's Diner in Spencer, just off Route 9, is very popular even though it is the new kid in town. It operated for many years on Plantation Street in Worcester before being displaced a number of years ago. The attached building with the dormers is a recent addition that houses the new bar and grill.

Charlie's Diner started out as Aiken's Mill Pond Diner in Wareham. The interior of this 1948 vintage diner is about 99 percent original (it is missing its Worcester Diner clock).

Blanchard's 101, to name a few). The lunch menu is also the dinner menu and has a huge selection of sandwiches (sides are extra). The soup and salad menu includes stew or chili and the soup of the day. There are garden salad, grilled chicken salad and a chef salad. There are sixteen dinner selections that run the range from ziti and Italian sausage to bourbon steak tips, liver and onions, meatloaf, baked ham and fried chicken, among others. Wraps are also represented (served with French fries) with marinated steak tips, turkey BLT, cheeseburger, tuna and shaved steak and cheese, as well as a Charlie's Chicken Wrap. The dinner specials ("Charlie's Predictable Plates") are listed by the day: Monday: roast turkey; Tuesday: roast beef; Wednesday: roast pork; Thursday: corned beef and cabbage; Friday: fresh seafood and macaroni and cheese; and Saturday: prime rib. Desserts are referred to as "Delectable Delights" and include a variety of homemade pies, puddings, custards, cakes, cookies, crisps and seasonal specialties. Take-out is available.

On the bar and grill side of the restaurant, the dinner menu is basically the same except that the sandwiches come with a side order of fries, etc. (the price is pretty much comparable to a sandwich and side, a la carte on the diner side). Operating hours are Sunday through Wednesday, 5:00 a.m. to 9:00 p.m., and Thursday through Saturday, 5:00 a.m. to 11:00 p.m.

BLANCHARD'S 101 DINER, CAMBRIDGE STREET, WORCESTER

Late 1950s uncompleted Worcester Lunch Car

Blanchard's 101 Diner is the newest late 1950s Worcester Lunch Car in existence. The diner, which finally opened in Worcester in March 2008, has been waiting to open since 1961 or even earlier. Let me explain. On May 23, 1961, the contents, tooling and other sundry assets of the Worcester Lunch Car and Carriage Manufacturing Company were sold at auction to Francis Van Slett. Mr. Van Slett, the owner of the Van Slett Sign and Advertising Company (also of Worcester), hoped to continue the long tradition of diner manufacturing for the city. He named his new enterprise the Worcester Deluxe Diner Manufacturing Company, keeping on some WLC employees, including Charles Gemme (the longtime foreman for WLC), who acted as a consultant. Later in 1961, Mr. Van Slett was quoted in a *Worcester Telegram and Gazette* article as saying that he was starting to build a diner on speculation, hoping that a customer would be forthcoming. Although Mr. Van Slett claimed he was building this, we now believe this was an unfinished diner

Blanchard's 101 Diner is Worcester's oldest brand-new diner. Construction on this diner was started by the Worcester Lunch Car Company in the late 1950s but never completed. It remained in storage for decades.

Here is the shell of the diner that would become Blanchard's as it appeared in the early 1980s. It was being stored inside a large garage owned by Francis Van Slett just off Park Avenue in Worcester. Van Slett bought all the assets of the Worcester Lunch Car Company at auction in 1961 and was the owner of Van Slett Sign and Advertising Company.

that Worcester Lunch Car had started to build back in the late 1950s that had been sold along with the other assets of the company to Mr. Van Slett. A prospective customer never materialized, so the diner remained in storage in a large warehouse until the late 1990s, when Van Slett's old property was cleared for new use. The building where the diner was housed all those years is still there.

At that time, the diner was moved to at least two storage locations— one in Fall River, Massachusetts, and later, another one in Rhode Island. But the structure, basically a wood-framed, plywood-sheathed box, was unfortunately largely unprotected from the weather for quite a while during those years. It sustained quite a bit of water damage and started to rot. This brings the story up to late in the year of 2005, when cousins Chris and Matt Blanchard were in the market to expand their family business known as Blanchard Foods (a vending and catering company). The expansion they envisioned included locating a classic diner and having it installed on their property to operate. They found out about the unfinished diner, then being referred to as Worcester Deluxe 101 (ideally it should be Worcester Diner No. 851), and felt that this diner, although just a plywood-covered shell, might just be what they were looking for. According to Chris Blanchard, this was sort of poetic justice, completing the diner that had been started so many years ago in the same city where it had originally been manufactured.

With Matt handling the construction, the Blanchards have done a wonderful job with what was essentially a blank canvas in the completetion of the diner. The diner now has four booths and a long counter with stools. There is indirect lighting along the perimeter of the wall at the ceiling, as well as recessed lights. The short-order cooking is done right behind the counter, with a large prep kitchen in the building behind. The exterior is covered with heavy-gauge metal panels (looking like flat extruded flutes) that were painted a pale yellow enamel in an auto body shop prior to being installed. There is stainless steel trim around the windows and at the roofline and corners of the structure. Due to the damage from being unprotected from the weather, the roof had to be shored up with three beams that were placed back to front and actually protruded below the ceiling height. The exposed beams were then covered with stainless steel trim and seem to fit right in with the interior decor. Blanchard's 101 Diner is operated by Matt and Chris. Chris is a certified executive chef.

Open every day for breakfast and lunch, hours are Monday through Saturday, 6:00 a.m. to 2:00 p.m., and Sundays and holidays, 6:00 a.m. to 1:00 p.m. Breakfasts include items such as "The Deluxe," featuring three eggs cooked to order with choice of bacon, sausage or ham and also a choice of French toast or pancakes. Other reasonably priced items are offered, like sirloin steak and eggs, a variety of three-egg omelets, smoked ribs and eggs, Italian breakfast and kielbasa breakfast. Egg and cheese sandwiches, pancakes, French toast and waffles are also on the menu, along with a waffle sundae and a huge selection of side orders for breakfast. By the way, they smoke their own ribs and pork right on the premises! Customers also rave about the homemade corned beef hash made with onions, ham and potatoes.

Lunch, 101 style, features mostly sandwiches (all served with French fries or home fries) such as turkey clubs, grilled ham and cheese, pulled pork and a variation called the Cuban. Hamburgers and cheeseburgers are here, along with a pastrami melt, Reuben, chicken cordon bleu and a steak and cheese sandwich. Other sandwiches include chicken parm on a bulkie roll, Italian sausage on Italian bread and meatball and cheese on a bulkie roll. Specials are available, like shepherd's pie, an open-face roast

Cousins Matt and Chris Blanchard bought the shell of the diner and finished the job that had been started many years before by completing the work on the diner's interior, as well as its exterior.

beef sandwich and various soups and chowders (by the cup or bowl). The parent company, Blanchard Foods, is a full-service catering company for various functions such as wedding receptions, bridal showers, banquets and meetings.

MISS MENDON DINER, 16 UXBRIDGE ROAD, MENDON

1950 Worcester Lunch Car

The newly refurbished Miss Mendon Diner had its grand opening on January 20, 2010. The Miss Mendon Diner, a beautifully maintained Worcester Lunch Car (No. 823), had spent the first fifty years of its operating life way up in the area of Vermont known as the Northeast Kingdom, in the town of Newport. Hard by the Canadian border, the diner's bright red porcelain-enameled steel panels were emblazoned with the name Miss Newport.

It closed in Vermont a number of years ago (about 2000) and was subsequently sold to Dave Pritchard of Salisbury, Massachusetts, who had it transported to his storage yard in 2003. It sat there for a few more

Kevin Meehan, owner of the very large multi-brand auto dealership Imperial Cars, bought the former Miss Newport Diner and resurrected it as the Miss Mendon Diner.

This photo shows the Miss Newport Diner at its original location in Newport, Vermont, in August 1983.

years. Pritchard sold the diner circa 2008 to Kevin Meehan, the owner of Imperial Cars. Imperial is a multi-brand automobile dealership taking up a huge amount of acreage a few miles west of Milford, Massachusetts, on State Route 16. Meehan—who is locally famous for his auto dealership's TV commercials touting "In the little town of Mendon"—had the diner transported to his property. Meehan spent a considerable amount of money to set the building up on a new foundation. This included an addition with a good-size kitchen/restroom building that also has room for four more booths and a handicap-accessible entryway. Meehan did this place up right. He replaced the original porcelain panels that said "Newport" with newly painted panels that said "Mendon." The paint job was so good it really fooled me; I thought it was porcelain when I visited the site in September 2009. The interior of the diner got a sprucing-up as well, with a newly installed replacement ceramic tile floor that, though different from the original small blue and green ceramic tile, complements the natural woodwork that Worcester Lunch Car Company was famous for.

The addition that houses the four new booths also has the same tile floor but, more importantly, also has woodwork and booths that replicate what

The Miss Mendon Diner got a new ceramic tile floor and laminate ceiling panels, as well as light fixtures, prior to reopening in January 2010.

Worcester would have done perfectly. The whole place also features art deco light fixtures that seem to go well, even though it is not what Worcester would have used. The original stools have been stripped and re-chromed, making them appear brand-new. The large, capable and very friendly staff make dining here a pleasure. Breakfast is served all day, with a menu featuring the usual eggs, eggs Benedict, three-egg omelets and even a breakfast burrito. There is also something for people with a large appetite called "The Imperial Breakfast" that has two eggs (any style), two sausages, two strips of bacon, two pancakes, home fries and toast. There is also a dish called the "Miss Mendon Mess," which consists of a toasted bagel topped with corned beef hash and three eggs (any style) covered with a Dijon mustard cream sauce and served with home fries.

For the weight conscious clientele, there is a parfait available that is made up of fresh fruit, vanilla yogurt and granola. Breakfast items from the grill include biscuits and gravy, French toast, Belgian waffles, a short stack of pancakes and even an all-you-can-eat pancakes selection. The all-you-can-eat consists of starting with a short stack and telling your server to keep 'em coming! For a dollar more, there are also blueberries, cinnamon apples, bananas or chocolate chips to either fill your pancakes or top your French toast. Homemade bakery items include muffins, Danishes and croissants, as well as bagels with cream cheese.

Lunch starters include various soups of the day, chili and New England clam chowder. There are also appetizers like nachos, chicken wings (plain, teriyaki, BBQ or buffalo style), loaded potato skins, Miss Mendon round fries, sweet potato fries and onion rings. Salads are represented by house, iceberg wedge, Caesar and Greek, with various dressings and also additions like steak, grilled chicken breast and grilled shrimp. Sandwiches range from grilled cheese, sloppy Joe and tuna melt to Philly cheese steak and a meatball sub, among others. There is also a hot meatloaf sandwich and a unique variation called "Mom's Leftover Lunch"—a cold meatloaf sandwich served on buttered white bread with tomato and red onion. The hamburgers are named after Meehan's auto dealership and different model cars, including the Imperial Burger (a double bacon cheeseburger with Thousand Island dressing), the Fairlane Burger (a regular hamburger), the Camaro Burger (a cheeseburger), the Corvette Burger (a bacon cheeseburger), etc. There are three hot dogs on the menu. A regular dog is called the Bobby Socks (choose your own fixin's). Another one called the Varsity comes with the Miss Mendon's own meat sauce and celery salt, and still another called the Leather Jacket is topped with chili and cheddar cheese.

All the dinner plates are served with freshly baked dinner rolls and butter. The selections include meatloaf, stuffed peppers, chicken potpie, fish and chips, shepherd's pie, baked macaroni and cheese, ravioli and meatballs, buttermilk fried chicken and boiled ham, among others. You can also find the "Best Steak Dinner deal in the Little Town of Mendon," called Miss Mendon's Sirloin Special, which is a perfectly cooked twelve-ounce sirloin that comes with salad and soup, vegetable of the day and a choice of baked potato, round fries or brown rice pilaf. There is a kids' menu where all the entrées are $3.95. The entrée selections are chicken fingers, grilled cheese, hamburger, cheeseburger, mac and cheese, hot dog and peanut butter and jelly. These come with potato chips and a kid's beverage. There are also daily specials that are announced on the Miss Mendon Diner Facebook page (www.facebook.com/MissMendonDiner) and a specials calendar on their website (www.missmendondiner.com).

Beverages range from the usual coffee and tea to fountain soda drinks, juices and milkshakes and floats. There is also domestic and imported bottled beer, as well as house wines (chardonnay, cabernet and white zinfandel). The Miss Mendon also offers desserts like bakery fresh pies by the slice from Gaetano's of Medway (apple, pecan, chocolate cream, blueberry and lemon meringue). For a mere ninety-nine cents more, you can have it a la mode. Other desserts include double chocolate cake and eight flavors of ice cream, as well as banana splits, fudge brownie sundae, chocolate chip cookie sundae and one called "Miss Mendon's Kitchen Sink."

Operating hours for the Miss Mendon Diner are Monday through Sunday, 6:00 a.m. to 10:00 p.m. In good weather, there is outdoor seating available.

BLUE MOON DINER, MAIN STREET, GARDNER

1949 Worcester Lunch Car

The Blue Moon Diner of Gardner started out life in Winchendon, the next town over from Gardner. It was known as the Miss Toy Town Diner when it was delivered there on April 4, 1949, to Arthur L. Bernier. From all accounts, Mr. Bernier moved the Miss Toy Town to Gardner in 1964 to replace another diner he operated there. That diner was a 1929 vintage Worcester Lunch Car known as the Blue Moon Coffee Shop. The Miss Toy Town was renamed Bernier's Diner and operated under that name for a number of years before it closed. It has been reported to have remained closed until 1976, when a local police officer named Robert Daneault reopened it as the Blue Moon

The porcelain-enameled panels now say "Blue Moon," but this diner originally came out of the Worcester Lunch Car factory in 1949 with the name "Miss Toy Town." Its first operating location was in nearby Winchendon, and it was brought to Gardner to replace a 1929 vintage diner known as the Blue Moon Coffee Shop in 1964.

Diner. The diner went through a series of at least three other owners until Dennis "Skip" Scipione purchased it in 1984. Skip brought the diner back from oblivion with a major cleanup of the restaurant, physically as well as spiritually, restoring its heart, soul and reputation in the process. About 1988, Skip wanted to replace the T-111 wooden panels that had covered over the spot on the front that once had the name "Miss Toy Town" on it. So he contacted Richard Gutman about the possibility of having new porcelain-enameled steel panels designed to have the name "Blue Moon" emblazoned across the front. Dick designed the three new panels that were made by Cherokee Porcelain Enamel Company, and they were installed in short order.

Skip continued to operate the diner, with a short break in the 1990s when he tried to retire. The person he leased the diner to was not able to keep the pace and quality of business, so Skip stepped back in until the year 2000, when he sold the diner to Jamie Floyd, a local waitress who wanted to run her own business. I met Jamie in 2001 at a meeting of the Massachusetts Historical Commission in Boston. This was when the Blue Moon was included in a group of diners being nominated to the National Register of Historic Places.

The interior of the Blue Moon Diner is 100 percent original, pretty much the way it came out of the factory. This diner is a must-stop if you are ever in the area. Owner Jamie Floyd always has a big smile, as well as great food, for all her customers.

Jamie and I were invited guests to the proceedings, where we both voiced our approval (along with other interested parties) of the handful of diners being added to Massachusetts Multiple Listing of Diners to the Historical Register.

Since Jamie has taken over, she has done an excellent job of keeping this local landmark going. She will always greet you with a big smile, great service and delicious food. If you are lucky, you will probably catch her singing along with the background music that is playing. Again, this is one diner I wish I lived closer to. Breakfasts are big here, with all the usual eggs, omelets, French toast and pancakes. Jamie also has a great breakfast special available Monday through Friday: two eggs, home fries and toast, all for just $2.00. Lunch specials include the Working Person: a fresh cold sandwich, chips and apple for $3.00. There are daily $7.25 hot lunch specials, which include roast pork, roast turkey, pot roast, chicken potpie and meatloaf, as well as fried haddock on Fridays. All these specials come with two sides; soup and dessert are $2.00 more. The Blue Moon Diner is open seven days a week, Monday through Friday, 6:00 a.m. to 2:00 p.m., Saturday and Sunday 6:00 a.m. to 1:00 p.m. On Thanksgiving and Easter, the diner is open for breakfast only, 7:00 a.m. to 11:00 a.m., and it is closed on Christmas.

Chapter 5

Western Massachusetts

Although this region of Massachusetts is fairly rural, it is punctuated with large cities like Springfield, Holyoke, Westfield, Northampton, Pittsfield, Greenfield, Williamstown and North Adams. There are also many colleges and universities in the area, including the University of Massachusetts, Hampshire College, Smith College and Amherst College in the vicinity of Amherst and Northampton, as well as the Massachusetts College of Liberal Arts in North Adams, Williams College in Williamstown and Berkshire Community College in Pittsfield. So basically, the diners in this area hold primarily to the large towns and cities, with a few exceptions. These exceptions include Chicopee, which historically was a mill town that also housed a U.S. Air Force Base (Westover), so there are diners located near the air base (Bernie's Dining Depot) and closer to downtown (Al's Restaurant). Palmer was also a small mill town that still has one downtown diner, the Day and Night Diner. On U.S. Route 20 in Wilbraham, on the eastern outskirts of Springfield, the 1960s vintage DeRaffele-built diner currently operating as Pizza Pub–Gregory's Restaurant is heavily disguised but originally operated at this location as K's Diner. Right off Interstate 91 between Northampton and Greenfield is a truck stop diner called the Whately Diner Fillin' Station. One of the newest and largest diners in the state came to Hadley (near Amherst) in the year 2000. Built by Kullman Industries and originally named the Sit Down Diner, this large, retro, stainless steel and enameled striped diner currently operates as the Route 9 Diner and seats 140 patrons. This region also includes a notable on-site diner called the Shady Glen Restaurant in Turners Falls and a storefront-type diner in the town of Lee called Joe's Diner. Joe's is famous as the place that was used as a backdrop in the Norman Rockwell painting titled *The Runaway*.

LIST OF DINERS IN REGION

Adrien's Diner
145 Wahconah Street, Pittsfield
Sterling Diners

Al's Restaurant
14 Yelle Street, Chicopee
Master Diners

Bernie's Dining Depot
749 James Street, Chicopee
Jerry O'Mahony Diners

Bluebonnet Diner
324 King Street, Northampton
Worcester Lunch Car Company (No. 825)

Charlie's (Charles) Diner
218 Union Street, West Springfield
Fodero Diners

Day & Night Diner
1456 North Main Street, Palmer
Worcester Lunch Car Company (No. 781)

Joe's Diner
165 Center Street, Lee
On-site

Kathy's Diner
6 Strong Avenue, Northampton
Worcester Lunch Car Company (No. 702)

Miss Adams Diner
53 Park Street, Adams
Worcester Lunch Car Company (No. 821)

Miss Florence Diner
99 Main Street, Florence
Worcester Lunch Car Company (No. 775)

Pizza Pub–Gregory's Restaurant
2391 Boston Road (U.S. Route 20), Wilbraham
1960's DeRaffele Diners

Route 66 Diner
950 Bay Street, Springfield
Mountain View Diners (No. 532)

Route 9 Diner
458 Russell Street, Hadley
Kullman Diners

Shady Glen Restaurant
7 Avenue A, Turners Falls
On-site

Whately Diner Fillin' Station
372 State Road, Whately
Kullman Diners

ROUTE 66 DINER, 950 BAY STREET, SPRINGFIELD

1957 Mountain View Diner

At one time, there were many diners located in the city of Springfield, but now the Route 66 Diner is the last one operating within the city limits. When this Mountain View Diner came from the factory in 1957, it was known as the New Bay Diner. One of the last diners to come out of the factory in Singac, New Jersey, its production number is 532. It remained operating under that name and in pretty much original condition right into the 1980s.

Springfield at one time had many diners, but the Route 66 Diner on Bay Street is the last one left in Springfield proper, although West Springfield, across the river, still has the Charles Diner (aka Charlie's). Originally known as the New Bay Diner, this is reportedly one of the last diners manufactured by the Mountain View Company.

The inside of the Route 66 Diner is very clean and looks to be close to original condition.

When brothers Don and Norman Roy bought the diner in 1985, they gave it some tender loving care, along with some new equipment and a good cleaning. One of the changes they made was to remove a stick-built entryway and have a new glass-walled vestibule installed in its place.

Open only for breakfast and lunch, the menu surprisingly has something for everyone. Breakfast is served anytime of the day and features a typical lineup (with some surprises) of eggs, home fries and toast with sides of bacon, breakfast sausage or sausage patty, as well as grits, kielbasa, hash, ham, bologna and hot beef or turkey sausage. Pancakes are served plain or with chocolate chips or blueberries, and there is also Texas toast (thick French toast), as well as Belgian waffles. There are morning specials like Eggs Irish (two poached eggs over hash on an English muffin, topped with cheddar cheese, home fries or grits), as well as Home Fries Supreme (two eggs, toast, home fries with onions, peppers, breakfast sausage, topped with cheddar cheese). There are also steak specials and build-your-own specials. Three-egg omelets and breakfast sandwiches are also offered, along with a large selection of side orders like homemade cornbread, water rolls, muffins and bagels, as well as salmon patties and country fried steak.

The lunch and dinner menu is as extensive as the breakfast offerings, featuring plenty of sandwiches and melts, as well as $1/3$-pound and $1/2$-pound burgers and cheeseburgers. There are also burger platters, hot dogs and chili dogs, as well as a selection of grinders and club sandwiches. Dinners are served with vegetable of the day and bread and butter for selections such as hamburg steak, hot open-faced turkey or roast beef, liver, meatloaf, pepper steak, country fried steak and boneless pork chops. There are two big steak lovers' dinners: a large sirloin steak with mushrooms, onions and gravy and a ribeye with mushrooms, onions and gravy. Seafood dinners such as fish and chips, clam strip dinner or fried shrimp dinner are available, along with a fish sandwich platter. Operating hours are Monday through Saturday, 6:00 a.m. to 3:00 p.m., and Sundays, 6:00 a.m. to 2:00 p.m.

Miss Adams Diner, Park Street, Adams

1950 Worcester Lunch Car

The first time I came upon the Miss Adams Diner, it was during a freak snowstorm in November 1982. I knew there had been a diner located in the town of Adams and wanted to see if it was still there and operating. Well, it

Even though the Miss Adams Diner acquired a stone façade at some point prior to 1980, the interior remained fairly intact until the last twelve years. Since then, its owners and sometimes operators have made some bad decisions, especially with regard to the inside of the diner.

was still there but was trading as the Pier 53 Restaurant. Sometime prior to my visit, the porcelain-enameled façade had been covered with a stone face. Other than that, it still looked pretty much like the 1950 vintage Worcester Lunch Car (No. 821) that it was. The interior was fairly intact, more so than the outside appearance would lead one to believe. It remained operating as Pier 53 Restaurant until 1988, when Barry and Nancy Garton breathed life back into the place. Renaming it the Miss Adams, the Gartons had a very successful run for eleven years. Unfortunately, the person they sold the diner to in 1999 basically became an absentee landlord who leased the building to a string of operators over the next eight or nine years. These operators mostly failed to develop and keep a steady stream of customers.

When Ric and Philomene Belair reopened the Miss Adams Diner on February 15, 2010, they discovered that the previous owners and/or operators had raised havoc within the diner. The interior was covered in paneling, with seashells painted on some walls and records glued to other walls. According to Philomene, there was no feeling of a diner within the structure. She said it was more like being inside a cardboard box. Ric and Philomene have since taken down the paneling on the walls to reveal the

The Miss Adams Diner's newest owners, Ric and Philomene Belair, have managed to stabilize a business that has been marginalized due to an absentee landlord who leased the diner to multiple operators. They are hoping to restore the ceiling by removing the panels that have been covered with old vinyl records, as well as make other improvements as time and finances will allow. As seen in this photo of the interior, almost all the original booths are still here, but the counter apron—along with the original ceramic wall and floor tile— was replaced somewhat unsympathetically by previous operators.

black-and-white tile half walls (not original). They also uncovered a previous attempt at 1950s nostalgia by removing paneling from the ceiling that covered the old vinyl records that had been glued onto the original Formica ceiling panels. Unfortunately, right now the records on the ceiling will have to stay. Due to budgetary constraints, any other restoration work has been put on hold until it is feasible to continue. Since opening, Ric and Phil have fostered a family atmosphere that has developed a loyal following. This family feeling was enhanced on August 21, 2010 (in honor of WLC No. 821), when Ric and Phil got married at the diner!

Breakfasts at the diner include the usual eggs (scrambled, fried or poached) and toast, as well as eggs Benedict, omelets, pancakes, French toast and waffles. Breakfast sides are typical, with ham, bacon, sausage, home fries and hash. Homemade muffins are available, along with diner specials including Scramble Station (three eggs with onions, peppers, cheese, home fries, toast and choice of meat), Diner Delite (three eggs, two meats of choice, home fries and toast) and the Number 821 (three eggs, two cakes, French toast or waffles, choice of meat, home fries and toast). One item that does not appear on the regular menu has become very popular at the diner. Philomene calls it "The Blitz," and it consists of an order of home fries drizzled with hollandaise sauce, and then a teepee is made with bacon, sausage and ham, topped with hash. Then, all that is topped by three eggs sprinkled with shredded cheese on top. Finally, two slices of French toast are cut in half and placed around the plate.

The luncheon menu features cold sandwiches, which include sliced turkey, sliced ham and roast beef, as well as tuna, chicken and egg salad. Hot sandwich selections include hamburger, cheeseburger, grilled cheese, hot dogs and BLTs. A Reuben sandwich is available, as well as a turkey Reuben, burger deluxe and turkey or ham club. There are starters like homemade soups (by the cup or bowl), chef salad, chicken fingers and fries and mozzarella sticks. There is a hot roast beef wrap with fries, as well as a pepper jack burger with fries. There is even a blooming onion available Fridays only (4:00 to 7:00 p.m.). Sides include French fries, onion rings and baked beans.

The Miss Adams Diner is open for breakfast and lunch Monday through Thursday, 7:00 a.m. to 2:00 p.m. Dinner hours are added on Fridays, when it is open from 7:00 a.m. to 7:00 p.m., and only breakfast is served on Saturdays and Sundays, 7:00 a.m. to 1:00 p.m.

THE WHATELY DINER FILLIN' STATION, STATE ROAD (ROUTES 5 AND 10), WHATELY

1960 Kullman Diner

The Whately Diner Fillin' Station is a true twenty-four-hour truck stop diner catering to truckers at Exit 24 off I-91. This is a Princess model built by Kullman Diners circa 1960 and was originally operated as the Princess Diner in Chicopee, Massachusetts. It was bought in the early 1970s by F.L. Roberts, a local company that has a chain of convenience stores, car washes and gas stations in the area. It moved the diner from Chicopee to Whately and ran it as the Maverick Diner for a time prior to renaming it to its current name. It is one of only a handful of diners that was built after the 1950s that made it to the Bay State. Its style could be called space age, with its large canted-forward plate-glass windows and flared-out roofline. Others have referred to this style as exaggerated modern, which is a fairly appropriate

The Whately Diner Fillin' Station is a great example of the space age diners being produced from the mid-Atlantic Diner manufacturers at the advent of the 1960s. With its large windows canted forward and flared-out roofline, it was one of only two diners from this period ever brought to Massachusetts that showed this futuristic styling.

The Whately Diner's interior is almost plain, but those fantastic light fixtures hanging from the ceiling really jazz it up nicely. I have never seen another diner with those fixtures.

term, as the diner manufacturers by this time had completely dropped the railroad car imagery of decades past in the design process. They were now highly influenced by a more modern aesthetic similar to what architects and designers were using in building coffee shops and restaurants that were big on the West Coast. This was all in the name of competition now that fast-food restaurants like McDonald's were making inroads into the family dining market. The old railroad-style look was passé. Kullman's Princess model is a highly refined example of this new look. Even the interior was up-to-date, with its *Jetsons*-style modern light fixtures hanging from the center of the ceiling. I have never seen light fixtures like this in any other diner.

Because of its convenient location off the interstate, the Whately Diner Fillin' Station, with its companion gas station, has twenty-four-hour facilities catering to long-distance truckers, featuring amenities like fuel, dining, showers, overnight parking, store, fax, ComChek and EFS. The diner has a fairly large menu aimed toward the truck drivers and other transient customers who frequent the establishment but also keeps the local family dining customers happy as well. The full menu is served twenty-four hours a day. The breakfast menu has items like the Traditional—two eggs with choice of bacon, ham or sausage (patties or links)—or you can add Canadian bacon for a little more money. Steak and eggs comes with either a four-ounce or twelve-ounce steak. Corned beef hash and eggs is also popular. The breakfast favorites include the Heavy Hauler, which has three eggs any style, two pancakes, bacon, sausage, toast and hash browns or home fries. Other favorites are biscuits and Gravy and eggs Benedict. Pancakes, French toast and Belgian waffles are available, as well as a selection of three-egg omelets, breakfast sandwiches and sides.

The lunch menu has a nice selection of appetizers, sandwiches and burgers. The regular burger is offered as either a quarter-pounder, quarter-pounder with cheese, half-pounder or half-pounder with cheese. There is a chili burger, Swiss burger, double Bacon Cheeseburger, garden burger (for vegetarians) and mushroom melt, as well as something called a Big Ben, which consists of a half-pound burger with cheddar cheese and bacon on a grilled English muffin. Everything from a clam roll, club sandwich, turkey Reuben and veal sandwich to a Philly cheese steak, tuna melt, French dip and hot sausage sandwich is offered as sandwich platters, all served with fries. Soups like French onion, New England clam chowder and homemade chili are offered, as well as the homemade soup of the day, by the cup or bowl. Various salads like tossed and chef are featured, along with a grilled chicken salad, steak salad plate, tuna salad plate and something a little out of the ordinary: a white salad plate, which consists of coleslaw, potato salad and cottage cheese on a bed of lettuce and tomato.

Dinners include everything from homemade meatloaf, chopped beef and a ribeye steak to fried chicken, veal cutlets, pork chops, stuffed turkey breast and butterfly shrimp, among others. These are all offered with a choice of two sides, including mashed or baked potato, home fries, French fries, potato salad, coleslaw, baked beans, cottage cheese, applesauce, pickled beets or hot vegetable of the day. There are some house special plates like a kielbasa dinner, franks and beans and spaghetti with meat sauce (add a choice of meatballs, veal cutlet, Italian sausage or chicken breast cutlet for a little more).

Desserts include puddings, pies and cakes (daily selection varies), along with ice cream (vanilla, chocolate, strawberry and coffee). There are also strawberry shortcake and a dessert waffle (a Belgian waffle that comes with ice cream and strawberries or chocolate sauce topped with whipped cream). They also offer kids' menus. A walk-up window serves ice cream cones, sundaes, shakes, floats and banana splits.

MISS FLORENCE DINER, MAIN STREET, FLORENCE

1940s Worcester Lunch Car

Florence is actually a section of Northampton, Massachusetts, located on State Route 9, just west of the campus of Smith College. The Miss Florence Diner (universally known as the Miss Flo) started out as a typically small, barrel-roof Worcester Lunch Car. Built for Maurice Alexander and delivered in October 1941, it was described as a fourteen-foot, six-inch by thirty-foot plain roof diner with seven windows across the front elevation and entrances at each end. It was covered with bright yellow, porcelain-enameled panels with the name "Miss Florence" emblazoned across the front, as well as the "Booth Service" legend on both front corners baked right into the panels. There was also built on-site a cinder block kitchen addition off the back of the diner. I am not sure how long the diner stayed like this, because at some point, Worcester came back and enlarged the dining car on location. The company accomplished this by extending the barrel-vaulted roof by at least ten to twelve feet on the right end and five to six feet on the left end. Worcester also made a rear extension to the new section on the right end, making the dining area L shaped, basically wrapping that side of the kitchen and making the Miss Flo a one-of-a-kind Worcester Lunch Car. I

The Miss Florence Diner is a real stunner, but that art deco neon sign on the roof really grabs your attention. The Miss Flo was altered on-site by the Worcester Lunch Car Company when it made additions to both the left and right sides of the original diner, making it longer. It also added the right rear section that wrapped the side of the kitchen for more seating.

would guess the fantastic Art Deco neon roof sign was installed at this time, making this already unique diner stand out even more visually, night and day. Eventually, the Alexander family connected the diner complex to the house in the rear and created a larger separate restaurant called Alexander's in the first floor of the remodeled house. Alexander's Restaurant featured a slightly more formal dining atmosphere with a full bar that served liquor. Operated by brothers Tom and Mitch Alexander, the diner was well known for decades and was always busy. People far and wide knew of the Miss Flo and the reputation it had for good food at reasonable prices.

By the early 2000s, the two brothers decided it was time to sell the business. Mitch wanted to retire, and Tom wanted to finally utilize his degree in pharmacology. The diner was eventually purchased by Konstantine Sierros, circa 2002. Sierros closed the diner briefly and made some changes by cleaning up the interior and replacing the original Formica ceiling with a wood-grain laminate. Other changes that occurred were the replacing of the countertop and apron, which were resurfaced in pink granite, and new wooden booths were added as well. Also, to bring the diner up to code for

The Miss Flo has also had some updating on the inside. This happened in the last ten years after the Alexander family sold the diner. New wooden booths and wood laminate ceiling panels were installed, as well as a granite face on the counter apron and countertop.

handicap accessibility, a new entryway was made, along with new restrooms behind the diner adjacent to the entrance of the former Alexander's Restaurant, now called the Silk City Tap Room. One thing had not changed; the ceramic tile floor in the diner was left intact. Walking into the diner through the front door, when you look down, you can see the seam in the tile where the original right end of the diner was extended.

Within a year, Sierros had turned the ownership of the diner over to John Zantouliadis, who has been running it for eight years as of June/July 2011. Upon my last visit to the diner in April 2011, the place was doing good business for 9:00 a.m. on a Monday morning. I was looking at the extensive menu and was thinking that the Miss Flo, along with some of the other diners located in Western Massachusetts, has a menu more comparable to Metro New York, Long Island and southern Connecticut than eastern Massachusetts. The quantity of items and selection was incredible. At the Miss Flo, breakfast is served all day, with classic items such as Miss Flo's famous corned beef hash and eggs, steak and eggs, ham steak and eggs, eggs Benedict, eggs Florentine and country fried steak and eggs (all served with toast and home fries), as well as something called the Breakfast Club. The specialty breakfast sandwiches are served on a choice of croissant, bagel, bulkie roll or English muffin. Omelets include a western, Greek, veggie lovers', meat lovers', three cheese, chicken, broccoli and cheddar, steak and cheese and a southern omelet. The Miss Flo features "Pancake Heaven" on the breakfast menu, which has nine different kinds of pancakes. Besides the usual plain, chocolate chip and blueberry pancakes, they have something called the Patriot (red, white and blue) and, for those patrons who are health conscious, multigrain pancakes. They also have some slightly unusual combinations of strawberry and banana, peanut butter and chocolate chip and banana and walnut pancakes, as well as one item on the pancake menu that sounds really decadent: strawberry cheesecake pancakes. Whoa!

The lunch menu at the Miss Flo is loaded with sandwiches, and I mean *loaded*! These include everything from cold salad sandwiches like tuna, egg and chicken to seafood items like fried haddock, fried scallop sandwiches and even a fried clam strip roll. There are thirteen items on the menu for triple-decker club sandwiches, as well as twelve varieties of eight-inch submarine sandwiches (with French fries). Hot open-faced sandwiches include roast beef, turkey, hamburger, pot roast, pork loin and meatloaf. There is a large selection of specialty sandwiches, including a French dip sub and Thanksgiving Day sub, along with Miss Flo's Reuben and a turkey Reuben. Various wraps—including California chicken wrap, turkey club wrap and Greek salad wrap—are served with either fries or coleslaw. There are four selections from the half-a-sandwich-and-cup-of-homemade-soup section on the lunch menu, including chicken salad, egg salad, turkey salad and ham and cheese sandwiches. Besides the sandwiches, the lunch menu features seven "mini dinners," as well as seven "mini salads."

The dinner menu at the Miss Flo has the usual appetizers like French fries and onion rings, along with other favorites including buffalo wings, boneless buffalo wings, mozzarella sticks, chicken fingers, fried ravioli, shrimp in a basket, hot poppers and loaded potato skins. Entrées include traditional diner favorites like specialty oven-roasted turkey, baked meatloaf, calves' liver, roasted pork loin, country fried steak and something called Red Sox Pot Roast. The butcher's block has selections like a ten-ounce prime rib, ten-ounce ribeye steak and broiled chopped beef hamburg steak, along with broiled pork chops and grilled ham steak. Italian dishes offered are spaghetti and homemade meatballs, veal parmesan, chicken parmesan and meat lasagna. Ocean-fresh entrées include fried haddock dinner, fried scallops, fried clam strips and fish and chips. Garden-fresh salads including spicy buffalo chicken or grilled Cajun chicken are offered, along with the usual classic chef salad and traditional tossed salad. There is also homemade chili and soup available by the cup or bowl, and various desserts are offered, including cakes, pies and puddings.

The operating hours at the Miss Florence Diner vary according to season. The winter hours are 6:00 a.m. to 8:00 p.m., and the summer hours are 6:00 a.m. to 9:00 p.m., seven days a week.

BLUEBONNET DINER, KING STREET, NORTHAMPTON

1950 vintage Worcester Lunch Car

The Bluebonnet Diner is one of only a handful of diners in Massachusetts that have been owned and operated by members of the same family for their entire existence. Since its arrival on King Street in May 1950, when it was bought by brothers James and Phil Greco, the diner has become a local institution in the Northampton area, known for home-style cooking at reasonable prices. Currently operated by James's son Jim, this diner is a unique design that was used three times in the 1950s by the Worcester Lunch Car Company, first for the Bluebonnet Diner (No. 825), then the Miss Beverly Diner (No. 828) of Beverly and finally by Arthur's Diner (No. 830) of Haverhill. This style of diner was small, fifteen feet by thirty-two feet, and had two entrances, one on each end of the front façade. These entrances had interior vestibule/windbreaks, and in between, there were four booths. It also featured fourteen stools at the counter, and it was attached to a kitchen/restroom addition built on-site off the back. The Bluebonnet has been expanded over the years, first in 1960 when the left-side wall was removed from the diner so there would be access to a decent-size dining room that wrapped the left side and back of the existing structure. This addition also housed a small banquet hall and lounge. With this addition, the Grecos had the removed side wall reattached to the left of the front door as an extension of the front of the diner, thus keeping the porcelain-covered walls and metal-framed windows to match the look of the original front wall. In the 1980s, the Bluebonnet was expanded even more when they added another extension off the left side, enlarging the dining room and also expanding out the back even more for the function facilities. According to the website, the diner with the expanded dining room seats 110, while the banquet hall (called the Florentine Room) accommodates 240 people. The diner, which got its name from the Texas state flower of the same name, has

Northampton's Bluebonnet Diner has been owned and operated by the same family since 1950. The diner, as well as the business, has grown over the years and currently features a large dining room, cocktail lounge and banquet facility.

The Bluebonnet Diner's interior has not changed much over the years. It features one of the largest menus of all the Bay State's diners.

remained fairly original, with the exception of newer light fixtures and the removal of the short-order cooking to the attached kitchen.

Serving breakfast, lunch and dinner, operating hours for the Bluebonnet Diner are Monday through Friday, 5:30 a.m. to 11:00 p.m., and Saturday from 6:00 a.m. to 11:00 p.m. The diner is closed on Sunday. Everything on the breakfast menu is served all day (except waffles). It offers the usual egg dishes, omelets, pancakes, French toast and waffles. The breakfast special is two eggs, any style, with choice of sausage links, sausage patties or bacon, home fries, toast and coffee, along with a small juice. Other egg dishes are offered with two eggs any style or one egg any style; these come with toast only. If you add bacon, sausage patties or sausage links, it will run $1.70 more, and $0.99 cents more if you want home fries. All the three-egg omelets are served with home fries and choice of toast. There are also four kinds of two-egg scramblers that come with toast; again, if you want home fries, it will cost extra. The Bluebonnet also offers sirloin steak with two eggs and grilled cube steak with two eggs; both come with home fries and toast. There are plain, blueberry, apple and chocolate chip pancakes, along with Texas-style French toast and a traditional waffle (additional waffles are $1.99 each). All are served with pure 100 percent Massachusetts maple syrup. Breakfast sandwiches include a fried egg sandwich; fried egg with bacon, ham or sausage; sausage patty on an English muffin; or sausage patty and egg on an English muffin. Bagels, plain or with jelly or cream cheese, are featured, along with homemade muffins, assorted doughnuts, grilled hard rolls and English muffins. Raisin roast, white, wheat and rye are choices as well. Cold cereals and hot oatmeal round out the breakfast menu.

Certainly, the breakfast menu is more than adequate, but the Bluebonnet really shines with the lunch and dinner menu. Here we can see that the offerings are fairly extensive, with everything from appetizers and side orders to salads and hot wraps, sandwiches (hot and cold), roasts and various other dinners. Appetizers include shrimp cocktail, baked stuffed mushroom caps and fried mushroom caps, along with the more typical fried mozzarella sticks, potato skins, chicken tenders and boneless hot wings. Side orders include French fries, onion rings, a side of spaghetti and tossed salad. More substantial salads like chef salad, grilled chicken salad and chicken tender salads are served, as well as a lobster salad plate, chicken salad plate, egg salad plate and a tuna salad platter. Homemade soup of the day comes by the cup, bowl and jumbo bowl. There is also tortellini soup and oyster stew available. Bluebonnet hot wraps include a hot vegetable wrap, chicken stir fry wrap and shaved Philly steak wrap, all served on a honey wheat tortilla.

Hot sandwiches include Italian meatball, veal cutlet and chicken cutlet. Seafood sandwiches include filet of fish (haddock), lobster salad roll, lobster salad sandwich, fried clam roll or fried scallop roll. Grilled sandwiches offered are eastern, western, grilled cube steak, grilled kielbasa, grilled cheese (add tuna, bacon or ham for a little more) and grilled hot dog. French fries or coleslaw are extra with these sandwiches. The sandwich selections continue with specialty sandwiches such as French dip, chicken parmesan, BBQ chicken breast cutlet and grilled chicken sandwich, all served with French fries. Burger selections are represented by the classic burger, classic cheeseburger, Luckyburger (¼-pound), Bar-B-Q Lucky and Lucky Special (with lettuce, tomato, pickles, onion and mayo). You can also create a burger basket by adding either French fries or coleslaw for $1.59 more.

The Bluebonnet offers three selections of stuffed croissants—tuna salad, chicken salad and baked ham and cheese—all served with fries. The eight varieties of triple-decker club sandwiches are stacked high on a choice of toast with bacon, lettuce, tomato and mayo (served with French fries). To round out this part of the menu, there are also deli-style sandwiches and wraps. Deli-style sandwich selections range from chicken, egg, ham or tuna salad to liverwurst, roast beef, roast ham and roast turkey. There are also boiled ham, hot pastrami bacon, lettuce and tomato and Canadian bacon, lettuce and tomato. Any sandwich on the regular menu can be made into a wrap with lettuce, tomato, onion, cheese and mayo on a honey wheat tortilla for $1.59 more. For the same amount, you can add French fries or coleslaw to create a sandwich basket.

The dinner menu features the Bluebonnet's famous house specialty—broasted chicken. This is cooked to order and comes in your choice of three or four pieces (served with two sides), as well as three-piece or four-piece chicken and spaghetti. There is an all-white meat available for an additional $1.29. Choice steaks served with two sides include New York strip steak (ten ounce and fourteen ounce) and a teriyaki steak (ten ounce). The roast dinners (roasted daily) include roast prime rib of beef, roast top round of beef, roasted stuffed turkey, roasted stuffed loin of pork, roasted stuffed half chicken and a half broiled chicken and are served with two sides. Seafood selections (served with two sides, roll and butter unless otherwise noted) include fried or broiled filet of haddock, fried clams (whole belly), fried or broiled deep sea scallops, broiled swordfish steak, fantail shrimp, fish cakes (add either baked beans or two sides for an additional $1.00) and lobster chunks in butter. There is also a fisherman's platter with clams, scallops, haddock and shrimp. Items from the grill include grilled chicken breast, grilled hamburger steak, grilled pork chops, grilled kielbasa, grilled beef liver, grilled cube steak and grilled Virginia ham steak, all served with rolls and butter and two sides. Grilled franks are also available with brown bread and baked beans.

The Bluebonnet's bakery features a great selection of pies: chocolate cream, banana cream, coconut cream, pineapple cream, apple, blueberry, cherry and rhubarb, among others. You can also order (in advance) whole pies to go. Other desserts featured include homemade puddings like Grapenut, rice, bread and tapioca, as well as sugar-free Jell-O with whipped cream. Pineapple upside down cake is available, along with a selection of layer cake, cheesecake, pecan pie and chocolate brownie (a la mode for a little more).

If this menu wasn't already huge, they also offer different daily specials Monday through Saturday. These specials are too numerous to list (each day has its own selections, from sandwiches to dinners, desserts and more).

Route 9 Diner, Russell Street (Route 9) , Hadley

2000 Kullman Diner

The Route 9 Diner in Hadley is the first new diner delivered to Massachusetts by one of the old-line diner manufacturers since the 1960s. This multi-sectioned diner consisting of seven modules built by Kullman Industries was delivered in March 2000. Totaling 4,200 square feet with seating for 140, this is certainly the largest diner ever built for the Massachusetts market. It came from the Kullman factory all done up in horizontal bands of satin-finish stainless steel with blue and red stripes. There is also a blue "top-cap" at the roofline that hides the HVAC equipment. Originally owned and operated by James and Susan Tourtillotte, the diner was known as the Sit Down Diner. From what I heard, Kullman wanted to use mirror-finish stainless steel on this diner, but the Tourtillottes insisted on the satin finish, as it was the type used on 1950s diners. The Tourtillottes had been operating a 1985 vintage Colonial-style Kullman Diner (also called the Sit Down Diner) in Danbury, Connecticut, for about a year prior to taking delivery of the new retro stainless steel model. When the new diner was being transported to Massachusetts, it spent its last night of the trip in the parking lot of the Whately Diner Fillin' Station located about fifteen miles away. Ironically, the Whately Diner was the last brand-new Kullman Diner delivered to the state,

The Route 9 Diner is the largest diner ever delivered to Massachusetts. It is modeled after the diners that were built in the 1950s but with a completely updated look.

circa 1960. Unfortunately, within two and a half years or so the Tourtillottes ended up having financial problems and defaulted on the mortgages of both diners. Kullman Industries bought back the new diner in Hadley at auction and, in fairly short order, found a new owner for this business in 2003.

When I last visited the diner in April 2011, I met the new owners, partners Chris Karabetsos and Archie Sideris. They were both very cordial to me and were eager to talk about their diner. I mentioned how I was familiar with the diner when it had been the Sit Down and that this was my first visit under the new ownership. I was told Chris was the person who took over the diner in 2003 and Archie, an old friend, came in a year later as a partner. They each have an extensive background in the restaurant and food service industry, and from what I have been told, you can always find one (or both) of them working at the diner, either back in the kitchen or out in the diner/dining room alongside their capable staff. As quoted from their website: "Chris and Archie believe in making food from scratch with emphasis on consistency, value & flavors." Their menu is extensive and very eclectic. They feature breakfast fare ranging from the simple egg and bacon to eye-popping challah French toast and huevos rancheros. Lunches and dinners cater to the comfort foods of meatloaf and turkey dinners and flip

The interior of the Route 9 Diner features ceramic floor tile, wood grain laminate benches and wall panels, as well as plenty of stainless steel and neon.

the switch to decadent Italian sauté and Greek specialties. Their longtime friend manager/baker Dimitrios Demos is responsible for the homemade desserts the diner is famous for. .

This diner operates twenty-four hours a day, 365 days a year, making it (along with the Whately Diner) one of only two diners in the state that never close. Like its close neighbors the Miss Florence Diner and the Bluebonnet Diner, the Route 9 Diner has an extremely large menu with something to please anyone's taste. The breakfast menu features the usual egg dishes (one or two eggs any style) served with home fries and toast, along with the regular choices of bacon, ham or sausage as sides. Other side meats include sirloin steak, ham steak, homemade corned beef hash and fried Polish kielbasa. Specialty egg dishes include huevos rancheros, eggs Benedict or eggs Florentine, as well as Irish eggs Benedict and a new addition called a Hellenic wrap. There are six kinds of what they describe as "Tasty & Fluffy Omelets": plain western, cheese, broccoli and cheddar cheese, spinach, Virginia ham and American cheese. There is also a new beef burrito omelet. Now those were just regular omelets; they also feature twenty different kinds of three-egg specialty omelets (too many to list). There are three healthy options for the specialty omelets: the Protein

Omelet, which is described as an egg white omelet with grilled chicken and spinach, served with cottage cheese; the Power Lifter, which is also an egg white omelet with all-white-meat turkey and American cheese, served with cottage cheese; and the Healthy Morning, an egg white omelet with spinach, broccoli, tomatoes and mushrooms, served with cottage cheese. All three do not come with home fries.

The selections from the griddle feature a dozen kinds of pancakes and eight kinds of waffles, all served with butter and syrup (add real maple syrup for $1.25). Cheese blintzes are served with sour cream or apple sauce, and they also have homemade potato pancakes. The Route 9 makes its French toast with its own fresh-baked challah bread, which is served with your choice of ham, bacon, sausage or Canadian bacon. They also offer a version with fresh strawberries and whipped cream. For something a little different, there is the challah bread French toast delight, topped with bananas, walnuts and whipped cream. For people with a big appetite, there is the Route 9 Special, which comes with two pancakes or French toast, two eggs (any style), two strips of bacon and two sausages. To round out the breakfast menu, they also offer assorted muffins, hard rolls, buttered toast and toasted English muffins, along with cinnamon toast, homemade challah toast and Greek pita bread. There is also a toasted jumbo bagel with a choice of cream cheese or Nova Scotia lox and cream cheese, or the bagel "all the way," with Nova Scotia lox, cream cheese, sliced Bermuda onion, lettuce and tomato. Breakfast sandwiches and assorted cold cereals, as well as hot oatmeal, are also represented.

If you thought the breakfast menu is huge at the Route 9 Diner, the lunch and dinner menu is even more surprising in its quantity of offerings. The appetizers alone have twenty-four different selections to choose from, from chicken fingers and buffalo chicken wings to fried or stuffed mushrooms, cheese quesadillas, cheese fries or chili cheese fries and disco fries. There is also crispy fried calamari, waffle fries, nachos, nachos grande supreme and something called a fried cheeseburger ravioli, among other selections. Homemade soups are served by the cup or bowl with saltines. There is also a crock of French onion au gratin and a bowl of chili con carne available anytime. There are fourteen selections of gourmet salads, including a classic Caesar salad, garden salad, spinach salad, Greek salad, portobello salad, buffalo chicken or teriyaki chicken salad and a Cobb salad. Salad toppings available include grilled or Cajun chicken, grilled salmon and grilled shrimp, for an additional charge. There are also cold salad platters like egg salad, tuna salad, chicken salad and whole jumbo shrimp, all served fresh on a bed of lettuce with tomato, cucumbers, potato salad, coleslaw, sliced egg and garnish.

The Route 9 Diner also has healthy delights on the lunch menu, including sliced breast of turkey, grilled chicken breast, tropical health platter and a black bean burger plate, as well as a Greek yogurt parfait. These are served on a bed of lettuce with tomato, cucumbers and garnish. The Route 9 Diner's classic sandwiches include a patty melt, tuna or turkey melt, Philly cheese steak, meatloaf sandwich and fried filet of sole. There is also something called a Breezer Burger, which is described as an open-face seven-ounce burger on grilled rye with Swiss cheese, grilled onions and a garlic horseradish sauce. These are followed by a Monte Cristo, grilled Reuben and clam boat, as well as a Balboa (an open-face hot roast beef on a toasted garlic hard roll). There are eight selections of triple-decker club sandwiches, such as sliced breast of turkey, grilled chicken and Swiss cheese and a Virginia ham and Swiss cheese, among others. All the classic and club sandwiches are served with French fries, coleslaw and a pickle.

There is a section on the menu called "Tasty Sandwiches"; these are served with coleslaw and a pickle and feature selections from the cutting board like roast turkey breast, roast sirloin of beef and roast Virginia ham. Corned beef or pastrami, as well as bacon, lettuce and tomato, are offered also. Grilled cheese can be ordered with a choice of American, Swiss or cheddar cheese, and you can have it plain, with tomato, or with ham or bacon. Tuna salad, chicken salad and chopped egg salad round out these selections. There are eleven selections of the "Route 9 Wraps," including Greek salad and chicken breast wrap, turkey breast tortilla wrap and crispy chicken honey mustard wrap. There is also a veggie Cobb wrap, all served with waffle fries, coleslaw and a pickle. This diner also offers a fine selection of eight grilled chicken breast sandwiches, featuring honey mustard chicken, chicken cordon bleu, Alpine chicken breast, Tex-Mex chicken, BBQ chicken, chicken teriyaki, California chicken and Southwest chicken. All these are served on a toasted bun with lettuce and tomato along with waffle fries, coleslaw and a pickle. There are also signature chicken cutlet sandwiches, all named after the area colleges: the Amherst, the UMass, the Hampshire, the Mount Holyoke and the Smith, as well as the Five College and the Undergrad. These cutlet sandwiches are served on a toasted bun with waffle fries, coleslaw and pickles.

Finally, the lunch menu has burgers! Yes, there are the Route 9 Burgers: a jumbo beef burger as well as a cheeseburger, offered in a regular or deluxe version. All the burgers consist of seven ounces of pure beef served with coleslaw and a pickle. The deluxe features lettuce and tomato along with French fries (as well as the coleslaw and pickle). If you don't want a beef burger, you can order from a choice of turkey burger, veggie burger or even black bean burger. There are also quite a few selections of specialty burgers, such as an Italian burger, Greek burger and chili burger, along with the lumberjack burger, pizza burger, supreme burger and seven more. To finish off the lunch menu, there are also hot dogs (kraut, chili and cheddar cheese are extra), as well as a chicken finger platter.

The Route 9 Diner is no slouch for the dinner menu either. Some of the highlights include home cooking entrées such as all-white-meat roast turkey with stuffing and cranberry sauce, roast Virginia ham with a fruit sauce, Yankee pot roast, homemade baked meatloaf, fried chicken in a basket and hot open-face roast beef or turkey sandwiches. The Route 9 also has homemade chicken potpie and baked macaroni and cheese. Then there are the sautés and Italian specialties, of which I'll only mention a few. There are items like chicken breast parmesan over pasta with marinara sauce and mozzarella cheese or chicken and broccoli fettuccine Alfredo and chicken Marsala. Other dishes include stuffed shells parmesan, seafood flamingo, sausage and peppers and zuppa de mussels, plus many more. Greek specialties are represented by chicken souvlaki on pita bread, a souvlaki platter, moussaka and a spinach pie. There is also a pastitsio (which is described as a Greek lasagna), a Greek gyro and a Greek combo plate.

Steaks and chops feature a sixteen-ounce broiled New York sirloin with onion rings, a sixteen-ounce broiled chopped sirloin of beef steak with grilled onions, mushrooms and peppers and two broiled center cut pork chops with applesauce. All three entrées are served with a cup of soup or Greek salad, potato and vegetable, bread and butter. "Fruits of the Sea" are the seafood choices of broiled, fried or baked stuffed items. These are served with a cup of soup or Greek salad, potato and vegetable, bread and butter. Broiled items include filet of sole with lemon butter sauce, fresh filet of Boston scrod and scallops. There is also broiled filet of Atlantic salmon with lemon butter sauce. The fried entrées include shrimp, scallops, clam strips and fish and chips. You can also order a fried seafood combo platter that comes with clams, scallops, filet of sole and clam strips. Finally, there is the baked stuffed shrimp with crabmeat stuffing, baked stuffed filet of sole Florentine with feta cheese and spinach and baked stuffed filet of sole with crabmeat stuffing and a lemon butter sauce. The Route 9 Diner also has two chef's special combos. These come with a cup of soup or Greek salad, potato and vegetable, bread and butter and are served in a lemon butter sauce (no substitutions). The first combo includes three baked stuffed shrimp and stuffed filet of sole Florentine. The second is called the Broiled Captain's Platter and comes with shrimp, scallops, filet of Atlantic salmon, stuffed tomato Florentine with spinach, feta cheese and stuffed mushrooms with crabmeat. The Route 9 Diner has plenty of side orders selections to go with your lunch and dinner, along with a variety of homemade desserts and international coffees, house wines and beer.

Chapter 6

My Personal Family Connection with Diners and Diner History

I have a unique family connection to diner history in Massachusetts. In the introduction, I mentioned how my longtime fascination with diners started in the mid- to late 1950s. My dad, Sam, was a huge early influence and source of knowledge in my burgeoning interest. Even though I credit my dad a lot for fostering my passion for diners, I cannot overlook my mother, Mildred, in all this. Over the years, she would mention every now and then about going to her cousin Tony's diner when she was a young girl. This diner, Tony's Café, was located on Main Street in Marlboro, Massachusetts. Shortly after Dad passed away in 1982, my mother dug out a circa 1930 photograph of her cousin's diner to show me. I immediately recognized the building as a place I had passed numerous times in the previous two or three years of diner-hunting trips as a place called D'Antonio's Diner. I had never photographed it, as to my eyes, this was not a factory-built diner but something that was built on site. (I was sort of a diner snob at that time.) Upon closer examination of this old photo, I noticed some details that I could not ignore. Embedded in the front wall of this small narrow building with a peaked roof was the remains of a horse-drawn lunch wagon! I was startled, to say the least. This was an amazing example of a rare and vital historical link in the evolution from lunch wagons to diners. Upon seeing this, I immediately went to my postcard collection and extracted two old sepia photo cards published by Underwood & Underwood showing the Monument Square area at the junction of Main Street, West Main Street and Mechanic Street in Marlboro. The views dating from the 1920s (my best guess) show from two different angles a lunch wagon in basically the same spot that Tony's Café (later D'Antonio's Diner) was to occupy.

Comparing the details of the postcards and the 1930 picture of Tony's, it was obvious that a window and wall section replaced the original door to the

Tony's Café, circa 1930, all decked out for the Massachusetts Bay tercentenary. My mother had this tucked away for decades, and I finally saw it in 1982.

Underwood & Underwood was a publisher noted for its sepia-tone real photo postcards. This first postcard view shows the lunch wagon that would become Tony's Café. It can be seen to the right of the automobile behind the park in the distance.

lunch wagon, while the window and wall section on the extreme right side of this same elevation had been removed along with the right end wall of the lunch wagon. These were replaced by a "slash-corner" door and shorter side wall, with one window that fit under the pedimented front overhang of the

This image is the same shot as a close-up, showing the lunch wagon much more clearly.

Here is the second postcard view of Monument Square in Marlboro. Taken from the opposite angle, the lunch wagon can be seen on the left.

This is a close-up showing the lunch wagon from the second postcard.

new building. A couple days after seeing the photo, I decided to take a ride out to Marlboro to revisit D'Antonio's. On the drive, I noticed that Steve's Place, a small Worcester Lunch Car that had been somewhat covered over, was torn down, and it looked like they were building a new road where the diner had been. Despite its disguise, I knew it was a diner as I patronized it once, back in 1972 when it was still in its original condition. I thought, "Oh too bad, they tore down the old diner!" Little did I know what was waiting for me in Monument Square. Yes, that's right, the road they were building came out onto Route 20 where D'Antonio's had been. I was stunned; two old diners gone in one fell swoop in the name of progress! According to Marcia Josephson, a clerk at the administration and engineering office of the Marlboro Department of Public Works, the plans for this Route 20 bypass around downtown Marlboro called Granger Boulevard had been in the works for a while. The city authorized land taking by eminent domain in 1981. Construction of the project was in 1982 and 1983, which would coincide with my little trip to check out D'Antonio's.

When I decided to write this story, I knew that I needed to get some backgound on Tony's Café, so I corresponded via e-mail with my mother's cousin John Gonnella, who has lived in the Los Angeles area since the 1950s. John's dad was Tony of Tony's Café, and he provided some background:

As to my dad's café, I remember that he purchased it from a guy named Moriarity. I have records showing my dad arrived at Ellis Island on October 19, 1921 on the ship Giuseppi Verde. *He went to live with one of his sponsers in Marlboro and went to night school in order to get his citizenship. I have diplomas from 1922, 1923, 1924, 1925. He went to work cooking for another café, I think it was called the Modern Diner which was located around the corner from the café that he was to buy in the near future. After he worked at the Modern Diner for a few years, he then purchased the café, I'm guessing now, but I think it was around 1928 and then re-named it Tony's Café. My mother would get in at 4:00 am and get things ready to open up at 5:00 am, along with one other cook. My dad would go into work about 10:00 am and worked the café until closing at 2:00 am. He would clean up the café and get home about 4:00 am, long hours. In 1945 he was having pains in his chest and stomach which at first they diagnosed as an ulcer. Later in the year he went to the Lahey Clinic in Boston and they diagnosed it as cancer and nothing could be done because it had gone too far. Around October 1945 he sold the business (not the diner/property) to Joe D'Antonio because he was getting too sick. He passed away at home on January 13, 1946. My mother passed away on*

Interior of Tony's Cafe, circa late 1920s. That's Tony Gonnella behind the counter. *Courtesy of John and Evelyn Gonnella.*

This is a later interior view of Tony's Café. It looks to be possibly taken right after the end of Prohibition, as there are signs advertising beer. There is Tony and his wife, Rena, standing in the middle of the photo. *Courtesy of John and Evelyn Gonnella.*

October 4, 1953 and the café property stayed in the estate until around 1956. At that time the executor asked me if I was ever going to consider going back to Marlboro to work the café and I told him no. He had a buyer for the property, the same guy who was running it, Joe D'Antonio [who continued to operate it into the early 1980s, when it was taken for the Granger Boulevard project].

I followed up with a phone call to John after this initial e-mail, and during the conversation, he informed me that he had a couple interior photos of Tony's Café. I was immediately excited about this and asked him to get me copies, which he was kind enough to do.

So although I was a little too late to physically revisit my family connection to diner history, through postcards and photos, as well as the above reminisces of John Gonnella, I have at least been able to piece together the story.

Massachusetts Diners in the National Register of Historic Places

The U.S. National Park Service is the entity that administers the National Register of Historic Places. The honor of a listing in the National Register was for years the domain of historically significant buildings or properties, individually listed or as part of designated historic districts, usually from the seventeenth through nineteenth centuries and into the early twentieth century. The National Park Service had a certain criteria that basically stated nothing newer than fifty years old could be listed. In the late 1970s, there was a group of interested people who wanted to get the long-closed Modern Diner of Pawtucket, Rhode Island (a 1941 vintage Sterling Streamliner diner), listed in the National Register as a historically significant structure of the twentieth-century commercial roadside landscape that seemed to be fast disappearing. The Modern Diner was in danger of being demolished, as it was in an area slated for urban renewal. This group of preservationists ran head first into that "fifty-year-old" roadblock, as the diner at that time was only about thirty-five years old. This group was ultimately successful in breaking through this barrier, and on October 19, 1978, the Modern Diner became the first diner listed in the register. Since then, there have been upward of forty diners listed nationally, but for quite a while, Massachusetts did not have even one example listed in the register. That is, until the Massachusetts Historical Commission conducted a survey starting in 1997. According to consultant Kathleen Kelly Broomer, this survey created an inventory of a select group of diners representing different styles and ages at that time in the Commonwealth. From this survey, the Historical Commission created a Multiple Property Submission (MPS) to the National Park Service. The nominations were actually done in three stages (September 1999, November–December 2000 and November–December 2003), and ultimately, twenty-two Massachusetts diners were listed in the National Register. The following is a list of the Massachusetts diners that made it into the National Register.

Agawam Diner
166 Newburyport Turnpike, Rowley
Listed September 22, 1999 (Diners of Mass. MPS)

Al Mac's Diner
135 President Avenue, Fall River
Listed December 20, 1999 (Diners of Mass. MPS)

Al's Diner
14 Yelle Street, Chicopee
Listed December 14, 2000 (Diners of Mass. MPS)

Ann's Diner (now operating as Pat's Diner)
11 Bridge Road (U.S. 1), Salisbury
Listed December 10, 2003 (Diners of Mass. MPS)

Boulevard Diner
155 Shrewsbury Street, Worcester
Listed November 22, 2000 (Diners of Mass. MPS)

Capitol Diner
431 Union Street, Lynn
Listed September 22, 1999 (Diners of Mass. MPS)

Casey's Diner
36 South Avenue, Natick
Listed September 22, 1999 (Diners of Mass. MPS)

Chadwick Square Diner
95 Rear Prescott Street, Worcester
Listed November 26, 2003 (Diners of Mass. MPS)

Corner Lunch
133 Lamartine Street, Worcester
Listed November 15, 2000 (Diners of Mass. MPS)

Jack's Diner (operating as Lanna Thai Diner)
901 Main Street, Woburn
Listed November 22, 2000 (Diners of Mass. MPS)

Miss Florence Diner
99 Main Street, Northampton
Listed September 22, 1999 (Diners of Mass. MPS)

Miss Toy Town Diner (operating as the Blue Moon Diner)
102 Main Street, Gardner
Listed December 4, 2003 (Diners of Mass. MPS)

Miss Worcester Diner
302 Southbridge Street, Worcester
Listed November 21, 2003 (Diners of Mass. MPS)

Monarch Diner (operating as Four Sisters Owl Diner)
246 Appleton Street, Lowell
Listed November 28, 2003 (Diners of Mass. MPS)

New Bay Diner (operating as the Route 66 Diner)
950 Bay Street, Springfield
Listed December 4, 2003 (Diners of Mass. MPS)

The Rosebud (Rosebud Diner)
381 Summer Street, Somerville
Listed September 22, 1999 (Diners of Mass. MPS)

Salem Diner
70½ Loring Avenue, Salem
Listed September 22, 1999 (Diners of Mass. MPS)

Shawmut Diner
943 Shawmut Avenue, New Bedford
Listed November 28, 2003 (Diners of Mass. MPS)

Ted's Diner (now demolished)
67 Main Street, Milford
Listed November 29, 2000 (Diners of Mass. MPS)

Town Diner
627 Mount Auburn Street, Watertown
Listed September 22, 1999 (Diners of Mass. MPS)

Whit's Diner (operating as Lloyd's Diner)
184A Fountain Street, Framingham
Listed December 4, 2003 (Diners of Mass. MPS)

Wilson's Diner
507 Main Street, Waltham
Listed September 22, 1999 (Diners of Mass. MPS)

There were a handful of diners that were part of the original survey that did not get nominated to the National Register, including the Whately Diner Fillin' Station (Whately), Jake's Diner (Fairhaven), Joe's Diner (Taunton), Judy's Diner (currently the Lunch Box Diner, Malden), Lou's Diner (Clinton), Nap's Diner (currently Gracie's Diner, Webster), Pilgrim Diner (Salem), Portside Diner (Danvers) and Timmy's Diner (Framingham). With the exception of Timmy's Diner, which is currently in storage, these diners could ultimately be nominated at a future time if the owners or local historical commissions wanted to get the ball rolling. Charlie's Diner of Worcester (now Spencer) was ready for nomination but was in storage at the time it was to be nominated, so it was put on hold and could be placed in the register if the Turner family were to pursue this with the commission. Both the Central Diner in Millbury and the Edgemere Diner (now known as the Edge) in Shrewsbury were also nominated, but their respective owners rejected the nominations. As of 2011, even though the count still reflects the twenty-two diners officially listed in the register, only twenty-one diners remain, as Ted's Diner in Milford no longer exists. The Town of Milford owned the property that the diner sat on and needed it to construct an enlarged fire department headquarters. The town moved the diner out within a couple of years of when it got listed in the register. The diner was brought for storage to a section of Rosenfield Park on Route 85, where it would remain until they figured out what they wanted to do with the structure. Unfortunately, the diner (which basically was a shell of a building) was vandalized within a few months, and the town had no other option but to demolish it.

List of Diner Manufacturers

S imilar to classic automobile enthusiasts who are adept at knowing many automobiles by make, model and year of manufacture, so, too, do diner aficionados pride themselves on being able to identify which diner manufacturer built any particular diner and possibly the year in which it was built. To the untrained eye, one stainless steel diner looks pretty similar to another. In fact, I did a slide presentation a number of years ago that I titled "Is It a Fodero or an O'Mahony." Through this presentation, I attempted to show the similarities as well as the differences between not just those two diner builders but any manufacturers. I pointed out some of the design features that set one builder apart from another, the differences in style and workmanship that someone with an experienced eye can usually spot that help in the process of identification.

Ironically, in trying to identify which company built a diner, some of these details can sometimes get confusing. As an example, say one particular diner built by Mountain View Diners may have been taken in on trade by Kullman Diners. Kullman would have turned around and sold that diner as a reconditioned unit, but before doing so, it would have completely changed the exterior while possibly keeping the interior fairly intact. So now the diner aficionado comes along and sees a Kullman Diner on the outside and a Mountain View Diner on the inside.

Massachusetts can be credited with the birth of the diner-building industry going back to the late 1800s, with people like Sam Jones, Charles Palmer and Thomas Buckley leading the way with the burgeoning lunch wagon business. Historically, there have been more than sixty manufacturing concerns that were in the business of building or renovating diners over the years since 1872. Some of these started out building lunch wagons and evolved into constructing larger diners. The Bay State was long represented by the likes of the Worcester Lunch Car Company in Worcester and J.B. Judkins Company, the manufacturers of Sterling Diners, out of Merrimac. There were many more companies from New York and New Jersey that built diners, and quite a few of these diners were delivered and installed in Massachusetts. All the initial information on these companies is credited to the research of Richard J.S. Gutman.

The following is a list of manufacturers that have examples of their product still extant in Massachusetts.

WORCESTER LUNCH CAR COMPANY, 4 Quinsigamond Avenue, Worcester, Massachusetts. This was the premier diner manufacturer in New England, operating from 1906 until the assets of the company were sold at auction on May 24, 1961. The company built 650 units (lunch wagons to diners). It was a direct descendant of the T.H. Buckley Lunch Wagon & Catering Company, as well as the Haynes & Barriere Company. Worcester was noted for its fine workmanship and detail, with interiors featuring oak and gumwood woodwork with ceramic tile walls and counter apron. It was also known for its exteriors that sported porcelain-covered steel panels with integral graphics baked into them. Many diners found in northern New England were built by this company. Some prime examples are the Boulevard Diner in Worcester and the Breakfast Club Diner in Allston, a late model featuring a stainless steel, Formica and ceramic tile interior.

J.B. JUDKINS COMPANY, (Sterling Diners), 18 Main Street, Merrimac, Massachusetts. J.B. Judkins was a wagon builder for many years (starting in 1857) and was famous for its line of fancy wagons, landaulets and, later on, luxury automobile bodies. It switched to building Sterling Diners in 1936. A handful of the first Sterling Diners featured a monitor roof with clerestory vent windows. After those first few diners, the company modified the roof style slightly, and the style was sort of a cross between a barrel roof and a monitor roof. By 1940, it had introduced a fully streamlined model with a bullet nose on one or both ends. This Sterling Streamliner proved to be very popular, but the company closed shop by 1942. The Salem Diner in Salem, Massachusetts, is a prime example of a Sterling Streamliner. There are four other non-streamlined Sterling Diners currently operating in the

Commonwealth. The Catman Café in Mansfield and Andy's Rockland Diner in Fall River are both heavily altered Sterling Dinette models, while Adrien's Diner in Pittsfield is a larger Sterling Diner that has also seen some changes inside and out. Joe's Diner in Taunton is another example of this style.

KULLMAN INDUSTRIES, INC., 1 Kullman Corporate Center Drive, Lebanon, New Jersey. Kullman Industries was founded in 1927 by Samuel Kullman, who had been an accountant with P.J. Tierney Sons Diners. Then known as Kullman Diners, the company became a leader in the industry and was building diners well into the 2000s. Although the Kullman Company still exists, it no longer advertises diners as part of its product line of custom-built modular buildings. The Route 9 Diner in Hadley and the Whately Diner Fillin' Station are two great examples in the state from this company.

MOUNTAIN VIEW DINERS, Route 23, No. 20 Newark-Pompton Turnpike, Singac, New Jersey. This company had a stylish, well-built product. The company operated from 1939 until it shut down production in 1957. Betsy's Diner in Falmouth, Route 66 Diner in Springfield and the Patriot Diner of Pocasset are representative of 1950s vintage Mountain View Diners.

PATERSON VEHICLE COMPANY (Silk City Diners), East Twenty-seventh Street and Nineteenth Avenue, Paterson, New Jersey. This company started building Silk City Diners in 1927. Its first diners were barrel-roofed models similar to what Jerry O'Mahony, P.J. Tierney Sons and Worcester Lunch Car were producing at that time. Silk Cities were usually never custom-built; it only offered a stock model that could vary in size and color only. The company closed in 1964. Although never prevalent here in the Bay State, there are still two Silk City Diners still operating, Tim's Diner in Leominster and Lou-Roc's Diner in Worcester.

FODERO DINING CAR COMPANY, 136 Arlington Street, Bloomfield, New Jersey. Fodero Dining Car Company was founded in 1933 by Joseph Fodero, formerly the metal shop foreman at first P.J. Tierney Sons (1922–27) and then Kullman Diners (1927–33). Fodero Dining Car Company also went by the name National Dining Car Company during a short-lived partnership with Milton Glick (1939–41). During World War II, the company, like a lot of others, closed for the war effort but resumed building after the war under the Fodero name again. It was noted for its work in stainless steel from the late 1940s through the 1950s. It built many diners in many styles over the years, running the gamut from porcelain steel–covered diners early on to brick and mansard roof Colonial diners at the time it closed in 1981. The Charles Diner in West Springfield, Edgemere Diner in Shrewsbury and Agawam Diner in Rowley are Fodero Diners still operating in Massachusetts.

SWINGLE DINERS, INC., 300 Lincoln Boulevard, Middlesex, New Jersey. This company was started by Joseph Swingle in 1957. Swingle started selling diners after World War II when his wife Kay's uncle, Jerry O'Mahony, convinced him he could make more money selling diners than as a schoolteacher. Swingle went on to become the sales manager at O'Mahony and then Fodero before starting his own concern. In 1987, Joe Swingle informed me during a conversation that the first diner he ever sold was the 1948 version of Carroll's Diner of my hometown of Medford, Massachusetts. Swingle later went on to take that diner in on trade when the Carroll brothers, Maurice and Jack, bought their new L-shaped Swingle Diner in 1961. Swingle Diner Company closed in December 1988. Victoria's Diner in Boston is currently the only Swingle Diner left operating in Massachusetts.

P.J. TIERNEY SONS, 188 Main Street, New Rochelle, New York. This company evolved out of the Patrick J. Tierney Company, one of the early lunch wagon builders (1905–17). Known as "Pop," Tierney went head to head to head in the lunch wagon competition with Worcester Lunch Car Company and Jerry O'Mahony Company. After Pop Tierney's death in 1917, his sons Edward J. Tierney and Edgar T. Tierney continued their father's legacy and built diners from 1917 to 1933. The My Tin Man Diner in North Falmouth (currently closed) is a P.J. Tierney Sons Diner and is possibly the oldest diner in the state.

WASON MANUFACTURING COMPANY, Springfield, Massachusetts. This company was a subsidiary of the J.G. Brill Company of Philadelphia. Brill was a noted manufacturer of street railway vehicles that branched out into building diners in 1927. Wason Manufacturing in Springfield (1927–32), as well as G.C. Kuhlman Car Company of Cleveland, Ohio, built all the diners for Brill. Lynn's Capitol Diner is currently the only Brill Diner known to still be in operation.

DERAFFELE MANUFACTURING COMPANY, INC., 2525 Palmer Avenue, New Rochelle, New York. DeRaffele Diners was started by Angleo DeRaffele, a carpenter and later foreman for P.J. Tierney Sons. After that company was liquidated in 1933, DeRaffele and Carl A. Johnson (a former president of Tierney Sons) resumed the construction of diners at the old Tierney plant using the name Johnson & DeRaffele. By 1947, the company was owned outright by DeRaffele, and the name of the concern was changed at that time to DeRaffele Diners. Currently headed by Phil DeRaffele, it is now the oldest manufacturer of diners in the world. It has been in the forefront in the current trends of diner design and is proud to be carrying on the tradition. At one time, there were at least six DeRaffele-built diners in Massachusetts, but that number has dwindled in recent years. One of the most pristine examples is Al Mac's Diner-Restaurant in Fall River. Another diner, the Corner Lunch in Worcester, was originally built by DeRaffele but was altered by Musi Diners when it was brought here from Long Island, New York, in the late 1960s.

JERRY O'MAHONY, INC., 977–991 West Grand Street, Elizabeth, New Jersey. This company was one of the more famous diner builders out of the Garden State. Started in 1913, O'Mahony and his partner, John J. Hanf, built diners out of a small garage in Bayonne. Because of the quality of construction, the popularity of this company allowed it to become steadily larger over the years, outgrowing the manufacturing facilities four times and ending up at the address in Elizabeth. The company whose slogan was "In Our Line We Lead the World" built its last diner in 1956. Massachusetts has a few O'Mahonys still operating, two prime examples being the Shawmut Diner in New Bedford and the Mill Pond Diner in Wareham.

DINERMITE DINERS, 3414 Peachtree Road, Atlanta, Georgia. Dinermite Diners are part of the wave of retro diners that started taking hold in the 1990s. This company advertises that it started building diners in 1959, but it cannot be considered part of the old line of manufacturers. The quality of workmanship and style that I have seen from this company has no resemblance to anything that was coming out of the factories in the mid-Atlantic states in 1959. In fact, the first name I heard this company operate under was Module Mobile, Inc. in the mid-1980s, when it started advertising a model called the Happy Days Diner. The company reorganized about 1989 as Diner Group Ltd. And, by 1992, operated under the name Dinermite. The Jukebox Diner in Somerset is the only example of a Dinermite diner in Massachusetts. It dates from the year 2000. Dinermites are still being built today.

STARLITE DINERS, Inc., 323 Second Street, Holly Hill, Florida. Starlite Diners was started in 1992 by Bill and Donna Starcevic. Starlite initially offered three sizes of diners: a 52 seater, another slightly larger seating 82 and still another seating 102. At some point, they named the company Valiant Diners. Valiant built its last diner in 2004. In September 2005, Don Memberg, owner of a company called Modular Diners, Inc. of Atlanta, Georgia, obtained the rights to build Starlite Diners. According to Memberg, Dave's Diner in Middleboro is a Starlite Diner delivered in 1997 and was built by Valiant Diners.

MASTER DINERS, Newark-Pompton Turnpike, Pequannock, New Jersey. Master Diners never made a lot of inroads in the Bay State. In fact, to my knowledge, Master only delivered one new diner to Massachusetts. The company started building diners in 1947 and only lasted into the mid-1950s. It built a few different styles that were kind of unique but still had a classic stainless steel look that everyone associates with a 1950s diner. There are only two Master Diners currently operating in Massachusetts: Jim's Flying Diner at the Southbridge Airport in Southbridge and Al's Diner in Chicopee. Al's has been at the same location since it was brand-new, while Jim's Flying Diner was relocated from Rhode Island to its current location in the late 1980s.

Index

About the Author

L arry Cultrera is an archivist/ photographer of the American roadside, specializing in documenting the American diner through his photographs. He is a longtime member of the Society for Commercial Archeology (SCA). Since October 2007, Cultrera has authored the Diner Hotline Weblog (dinerhotline.wordpress.com), which is a continuation of a column he penned for the SCA's *Journal Magazine* for over eighteen years. He has been researching diners and their history since 1980, although he can trace his interest back to his childhood in Medford, Massachusetts. He has photographed and kept a running log (now a computerized database) of over eight hundred of these truly unique American restaurants and has a collection of memorabilia consisting of everything from postcards, menus, matchbook covers and business cards to toy diner models, T-shirts and actual selected pieces of now demolished diners, such as marble countertops, exterior panels, signs and light fixtures.

Mr. Cultrera has been featured on various TV shows that covered the subject of diners, such as *CBS Sunday Morning with Charles Kuralt* and *Bob Elliot*

Presents New England Diners (WCSH Channel 6, Portland, Maine), which also ran on cable TV's Discovery Channel. He has also appeared on WCVB-TV's *Chronicle*. He has been interviewed for numerous newspaper and magazine articles including the *Boston Globe*, the *Syracuse* [New York] *Post Standard* and the *Portland* [Maine] *Press Herald*, as well as *Smithsonian Magazine, Insight Magazine* and *Yankee Magazine*. He also conducts popular slide presentations on subjects such as the history of diners entitled "From Lunch Carts to Mega Restaurants, 1872 to the Present—The Ever-Changing Appearance of the American Diner," as well as one entitled "Local Roadside Memories," for various historical societies, art associations and other interested organizations.

Visit us at
www.historypress.net